"A jewel in the crown of any cookbook shelf, *Pitmaster* serves up a big-hearted dollop of authentic techniques as seen through the exacting, wonky, award-winning minds of a couple of Yankee barbecue freakazoids. This Ohio pitmaster cannot wait to smoke and grill his way through each and every gleaming recipe. Winter can bite me."
—JOHN MARKUS, EXECUTIVE PRODUCER OF *The Ultimate BBQ Showdown* AND EMMY-AWARD—WINNING WRITER

"Okay, now I'm hungry! Andy and Chris's superb barbecue techniques and amiable humor are all wrapped up into one pork-craklin' sandwich of recipes!"
—BEN MEZRICH, *New York Times* BESTSELLING AUTHOR OF *The Accidental Billionaires* AND *Bringing Down the House*

"Andy and Chris have combined all the elements for sharing the culture of barbecue. By embracing all regional barbecue styles and experience levels and flavoring liberally with their own expertise and acumen, they've captured the spirit of our community. Bon appetit!"
—CAROLYN WELLS, EXECUTIVE DIRECTOR AND CO-FOUNDER OF THE KANSAS CITY BARBEQUE SOCIETY

ANDY HUSBANDS
CHRIS HART

Pitmaster

**RECIPES, TECHNIQUES
& BARBECUE WISDOM**

Foreword by Amy Mills and
Mike "The Legend" Mills

FAIR WINDS

Photography by Ken Goodman

Brimming with creative inspiration, how-to projects, and useful information to enrich your everyday life, Quarto Knows is a favorite destination for those pursuing their interests and passions. Visit our site and dig deeper with our books into your area of interest: Quarto Creates, Quarto Cooks, Quarto Homes, Quarto Lives, Quarto Drives, Quarto Explores, Quarto Gifts, or Quarto Kids.

© 2017 Quarto Publishing Group USA Inc.

Text © 2017 Andy Husbands and Chris Hart

Photography © 2017 Ken Goodman

First published in the United States of America in 2017 by

Fair Winds Press, an imprint of The Quarto Group

100 Cummings Center, Suite 265-D, Beverly, Beverly, MA 01915, USA.

T (978) 282-9590 F (978) 283-2742 QuartoKnows.com

Fair Winds Press titles are also available at discount for retail, wholesale, promotional, and bulk purchase. For details, contact the Special Sales Manager by email at specialsales@quarto.com or by mail at The Quarto Group, Attn: Special Sales Manager, 100 Cummings Center, Suite 265-D, Beverly, MA 01915, USA.

21 20   7

ISBN: 978-1-59233-758-3

Library of Congress Cataloging-in-Publication Data

Names: Husbands, Andy, author. | Hart, Chris, 1969- author.

Title: Pitmaster : recipes, techniques, and barbecue wisdom / Andy Husbands
    and Chris Hart.

Description: Beverly, Massachusetts : Fair Winds Press, an imprint of Quarto
    Publishing Group USA Inc., [2017] | Includes index.

Identifiers: LCCN 2016049152 | ISBN 9781592337583 (hardcover book)

Subjects: LCSH: Barbecuing. | LCGFT: Cookbooks.

Classification: LCC TX840.B3 H8657 2017 | DDC 641.7/6--dc23

LC record available at https://lccn.loc.gov/2016049152

Writing and Editing Services: April White

Cover Image: Ken Goodman

Page Layout & Design: Landers Miller Design

Photography: Ken Goodman with the exception of page 40, Rob Bass; page 90, Steve Snodgrass; page 116, Andrew Bayda;
    and page 146, Creative Commons.

Printed in China

FOR
JENNY & RICE

Contents

4

TEXAS

5

THE NORTH

6

COMPETITION BARBECUE

Barbecue State of the Union

By Amy Mills and Mike "The Legend" Mills

This is the golden age of barbecue in America. In the dozen-plus years since our book *Peace, Love, and Barbecue* was published, barbecue has skyrocketed in popularity. Barbecue has emerged as a breakout cooking genre, earning respect for its intricate regional history and manifold methods and becoming a cuisine unto itself. Pitmasters are a new breed of rock star, folk heroes whose stories are kept in the spotlight by flocks of bloggers, reporters, photographers, and TV crews.

Mind you, barbecue is not the new cupcake. It's neither a trend nor a revival. The cooking and the culture — the food and the folklore and the feelings—are inextricably entwined and deeply rooted in heritage and history. And, like any worthy legacy, barbecue continues to evolve in the able hands and brave hearts of the next generation.

Many are the paths that lead to the pit. Like Amy, Sam Jones was born into the business and he embraced his heritage reluctantly at first. He's now the torchbearer of whole hog barbecue in North Carolina, carrying on his family's rich tradition at Skylight Inn while forging his own sterling identity up the road at Sam Jones Barbecue. Meanwhile, John Lewis, a native son of Texas and a pastry chef by training, now helms his own Lewis Barbecue in Charleston, South Carolina, and it seems like the whole world is scrambling to replicate his innovations in brisket and beef ribs. Tuffy Stone, one of the most talented chefs and pitmasters we know, has earned tremendous success on the competition circuit, on barbecue television, and

with his string of barbecue restaurants in Richmond, Virginia.

Then there are these two New Englanders, Chris Hart and Andy Husbands, whom we've had the pleasure to know for well over a decade. We've watched as they've continually tweaked their methods and honed their skills—no one cheered louder than we when their team, IQUE, became the first New England team to win the Jack Daniel's World Invitational Barbecue Cooking Contest in 2009. All the while, in true barbecue fashion, they haven't merely earned accolades for their food, but they've also embraced the people and the culture of barbecue.

Over the course of the decade or so we've known Chris and Andy, America has been to war, withstood economic woes, and weathered a full-fledged identity crisis. Our homeland remains fraught with deep and abiding uncertainty, and barbecue—America's original comfort food—nourishes the body and soothes the soul. Barbecue keeps us connected to what is good and wholesome and pure about our country—and it is about the people as much as the food. Folks are flocking to barbecue in search of sustenance and community; whether your barbecue is a backyard or restaurant or festival experience, it wraps you in warmth and belonging.

We're fond of putting it this way: Barbecue=food+family+love. In this treasure of a book, Chris and Andy highlight some prominent citizens of the barbecue world. Reading their stories and reveling in their recipes reminds us how very fortunate we are to be part of this great big barbecue family.

> *Barbecue continues to evolve in the able hands and brave hearts of the next generation.*

Preface

by Chris and Andy

We are a couple guys from Boston. Our grandpappys weren't cooking barbecue back in the early 1900s and neither of us stepped foot in the South until we were in our 20s. But we have been immersed in the barbecue life for the past 25 years. The spark came from a couple of restaurants local to us: a burnt-end sandwich at East Coast Grill in Cambridge, Massachusetts, and Memphis-style ribs at Jakes Q-for-U in Boston. We continued down the rabbit hole, traveling and opening restaurants and then dedicating ourselves to competition barbecue. These years of experience have culminated with Andy opening The Smoke Shop in Cambridge, Massachusetts, and Chris becoming the first pitmaster from the Northeast to lead his team to a Barbecue World Championship.

Since the publication of our first book, *Wicked Good Barbecue*, American craft barbecue cooking has continued to soar in popularity. Authentic barbecue restaurants are opening across the country, The Kansas City Barbecue Society has doubled membership, and barbecue message boards are teeming with newbies. Pitmasters are becoming bona fide celebrities. And most importantly, more people every day are turning off their gas grills and cooking with wood.

This book is about our barbecue paths—sharing what we have learned and focusing on the barbecue regions and people that inspire us the most. We have been influenced by barbecue restaurant owners with a commitment to regional traditions, competition barbecue champions, families with a multi-generational tradition of cooking whole hogs for holidays, and even amateur backyard fanatics.

We looked to barbecue author and television host Steven Raichlen and one of our mentors, barbecue legend Jake Jacobs, to provide the voice of the backyard barbecue cooks. Much of our inspiration starts with the traditional barbecue regions of North Carolina, Texas, and Kansas City. We've turned

This book is about our barbecue paths—sharing what we have learned and focusing on the barbecue regions and people that inspire us the most.

to our barbecue friends from those regions, such as pitmasters Sam Jones, John Lewis, Rod Gray, and Elizabeth Karmel, and pit builder Jamie Geer, for wisdom and insight into these American culinary legacies.

Innovation and tradition, though, are not mutually exclusive in the world of barbecue. We see essentially new regional styles developing in the North and out on the competition barbecue trail. Pitmasters Tuffy Stone and Billy Durney helped us explore what it means to both pay homage to traditional barbecue and infuse new ideas, flavors, and experiences.

The most important thing we learned from our own barbecue experiences and those of our friends is this: You need to trust your instincts. Barbecue introduces so many variables to the cooking process. What is the moisture content of the wood? Is the weather hot and humid or dry, cold, and windy? How is the marbling of the pork? There is a big difference in operation between a brand new tight smoker and one with 5 years of use and a slightly out of round lid. Great pitmasters focus more on what their senses tell them—the aroma of the fire, the appearance of the bark, the sound of crispy skin on a whole hog—than the exact temperature or time or proportions.

It is only after many hours of repetition that a barbecue cook is able to shift away from closely following a recipe as taught by a mentor or read in a book and move towards instinctive cooking, the ultimate mark of a pitmaster. The good news is there is no glass ceiling on deliciousness. No matter how far you are down the barbecue path, the time, care, and dedication required to feed your friends and family a plate of barbecue makes them happy. Making people happy is what draws us deeper into our barbecue journey. We hope this book provides guidance and inspiration as you continue down your own pitmaster path.

Backyard Barbecue

"The only real stumbling block is fear of failure.
In cooking you've got to have a what-the-hell attitude."
–JULIA CHILD

This chapter focuses on classic pitmaster recipes, staples, and skills you can use to get to know your smoker and consistently produce a great plate of barbecue. Eventually, you'll find yourself adding your own flavors and personality to the recipes.

If you are brand new to barbecue, turn off the gas grill and find a convenient spot in your backyard for a smoker. A Weber Smoky Mountain Cooker, kamado–style smoker, or Jambo Backyard model are all excellent choices for beginners. If you are not quite ready to invest in a new smoker, any charcoal grill can be used by employing the two-zone cooking method (see page 15). Other key pieces of equipment that you should have from the get-go are a charcoal chimney, a high-quality meat thermometer, and a dedicated coffee grinder for blending spice rubs.

Start simple and get the hang of how to maintain a steady temperature by cooking inexpensive cuts like a bologna chub or a few links of sausage. You'll probably ruin some meat but that's okay. You are experimenting with operating your smoker.

You also want to concentrate on burning a clean fire. You'll know you've achieved this when you see that almost invisible blue smoke wafting from your smoker stack. If you are producing billowing white smoke, your fire is smoldering instead of actively combusting. A fancy recipe cannot cover up issues with fire control. Clean charcoal, seasoned wood, and proper airflow are key.

Don't fear cooking hot. Most clean fire issues are the result of choking down the airflow to achieve very low temperatures in the 225°F (110°C) range. Chris's top piece of advice when he teaches his backyard barbecue classes is to cook hotter (275 to 300°F [135 to 150°C]). A hot fire is a clean fire.

Our primers on using the Two-Zone Cooking Method (see page 15), Weber Smokey Mountain Cooker (see page 16), kamado–style smoker (Classic Pulled Pork on a Kamado-style Smoker, page 25), and Offset Pit Barrel (see page 135) will help you get started, but there is no definitive way to maintain steady temperatures. It's about developing an approach that works for you.

Get started by throwing a party and cooking barbecue. Maybe you're not quite ready to cook for 30 people. But nothing beats experience, and you can always call the pizza shop if the pork butts just won't get done on time. And feel free to get creative. Will the beef rub work on a pork shoulder? Give it a try and let us know.

Even now, as more accomplished pitmasters, we have not moved on from these types of foundational recipes. We cook them again and again because they are delicious and our family and friends enjoy these dishes.

A fancy recipe cannot cover up issues with fire control. Clean charcoal, seasoned wood, and proper airflow are key.

USING A CHIMNEY STARTER

1. Place the chimney on top of a grill grate or other heat-proof surface with good airflow.

2. Place two sheets of crumpled newspaper in the base of the chimney and fill the top of the chimney three-quarters full with charcoal.

3. Light the newspaper and wait about 5 minutes.

4. When the charcoal is lit and flames are just starting to peek through the top, pour the lit charcoal into your fire chamber and get cooking.

ESSENTIAL BARBECUE EQUIPMENT AND TOOLS

Smokers we recommend:
  ★ Weber Smokey Mountain Cooker
  ★ Big Green Egg
  ★ Humphrey's BBQ Cabinet Smoker
  ★ Jambo Pits' J3 or Backyard Smoker

Fuel:
  ★ High quality, dense lump charcoal
  ★ Seasoned chunks of fruitwood, oak, and hickory
  ★ Seasoned split of oak, pecan, and hickory

Equipment:
  ★ Charcoal chimney starter
  ★ Fast-reading, accurate meat thermometer
  ★ Probe thermometer
  ★ A dedicated coffee grinder for blending spices
  ★ Meat injector
  ★ Nitrile disposable gloves
  ★ Insulated heatproof gloves
  ★ Grill brush
  ★ Silicone brushes
  ★ Spray bottle

TWO-ZONE BARBECUE COOKING

A requirement for almost all of the recipes in this book is cooking equipment that produces smoke and an indirect heat source. If you want to get started but haven't made the plunge and purchased a barbecue smoker yet, fear not. While you save up the scratch for your dream barbecue pit, you can use your grill. Yes, even a gas grill—but only if you promise this is a temporary thing.

To set up your grill for two-zone barbecue cooking, pile some unlit charcoal against one side of the grill. Light a chimney of charcoal and pour the lit coals over the top of the unlit pile. One side of the grill now has a charcoal base—the hot zone—and the other side should have no charcoal at all—the cool zone. If you'd like, outfit the area below the cooking grate on the cool side with an aluminum pan to catch the drippings of the meat. Set all vents to 75 percent closed and if possible position the exhaust vent above the cool zone. Place the meat on the grill grate on the cool zone side. Position a probe thermometer near the grate to measure the target temperature.

A high-quality smoker will run for hours without any fussing around with the fire. In a two-zone grill setup, however, you'll need to tend to the charcoal

base fairly frequently. Add a handful of charcoal onto the base every 30 to 45 minutes. Avoid letting the charcoal base burn all the way down or you'll need to start over. Optionally, add a handful of dry wood chips to your fire a couple times during the cooking process. Do not soak the wood chips. Wet wood will smolder and create bitter, off flavors.

For gas grill two-zone cooking, turn on only one burner. Depending on the grill design, use the back burner or the burner to the far right or far left. Wrap some wood chips tightly in aluminum foil and place them directly on the burner. Place the meat on the cool zone side and replenish with a new wood chip packet a few times during your cook. While your gas grill is doing its thing, go on the Internet and research which proper barbecue smoker you are going to buy.

USING A WEBER SMOKEY MOUNTAIN COOKER

If you are just getting started with a Weber Smokey Mountain Cooker (WSM), consider running the cooker the same way whether you are planning a two-hour chicken cook or an overnight pork butt cook. You may waste a bit of charcoal, but it's good practice to get multiple repetitions on a standard operating approach.

We prefer high-quality lump charcoal. "High quality" here is synonymous with the high density of brands such as Wicked Good Weekend Warrior Blend Lump Charcoal, Nature's Own Basque Hardwood, and Blues Hog Premium Natural Lump Charcoal. And we'll take a natural briquette over lightweight, cheap lump charcoal.

As with any bit of cooking, mise en place is essential. Start by organizing the following: lump charcoal, three fist-sized chunks of dry smoke wood, charcoal chimney, newspaper, probe thermometer, lighter, grill brush, heatproof gloves, and a large plastic plant watering can.

Fully assemble the WSM and then take the lid and the middle section off of the base.

Fill the smoker's charcoal ring with lump charcoal. For shorter cooking times, feel free to use less charcoal but lean toward adding more charcoal than you think you'll need. For overnight cooking, always start with as much charcoal as possible. Light a charcoal chimney (see page 15). When the charcoal is lit and flames are just starting to peek through the top, pour the lit charcoal over the center of the charcoal base.

Assemble the middle section onto the base and fill the water pan with water. Place the lid on the smoker and set all

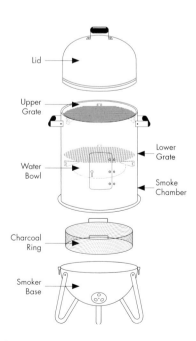

Lid

Upper Grate

Water Bowl

Lower Grate

Smoke Chamber

Charcoal Ring

Smoker Base

If you are producing billowing white smoke, your fire is smoldering instead of actively combusting.

vents to 100 percent open. After 20 minutes, brush the grill grates clean.

It's important to understand the smoker temperature measured near the center of the cooker at grate level. We use a calibrated probe thermometer pierced through half of a small onion sitting on the grate near where the meats are. If your WSM is outfitted with a lid thermometer, note what the lid thermometer reads in comparison to your probe thermometer. After a few cooks, you'll find the probe thermometer reads consistently cooler than the lid thermometer. Once you determine that difference, you can ditch the probe and use the lid thermometer as a guide to achieve your desired grate-level temperature.

Place the meat on your WSM. Open the access door and add chunks of smoking wood. Close the access door. Once the target temperature is reached, close the bottom vents 25 percent. Continue to adjust the bottom vents

to lock in your target temp. Be patient and make small gradual changes. Only close down the top vent if you have greatly overshot the target temp. Ideally, you'll be running with the bottom vents partially closed and the top vent 75 to 100 percent open. For an overnight cook, have a full water can and additional charcoal at the ready. Right before calling it a night, add some additional charcoal and top off the water pan via the access door.

When the cook is complete, close all vents 100 percent. The next day, dump and clean the water pan. With tongs, shake the charcoal grate to separate any ash from unused charcoal. Dump the ash and let the unused charcoal sit on the charcoal grate for reuse during your next cook. Reassemble the cooker and fit on the cover.

Memphis-Style Dry Rub Baby Back Ribs

How can you not love a BBQ joint that you to have wander down a dark alley in Memphis to find? Down a flight of stairs to Charlie Vergos' Rendezvous and back in time you go. There's nothing fancy about this restaurant—if you are looking for that new style cutting-edge barbecue, this is not the place for you. Get yourself a pitcher of Bud, order the cheese and sausage plate and the ribs, and enjoy a slice of the past. This is our tribute to that incomparable feeling.

Prep time: 30 minutes
Cook time: 3 hours
Serves: 4 for dinner

INGREDIENTS

2 racks of baby back ribs (3 to 4 pounds, or 1.3 to 1.8 kg)
¾ cup (75 g) Everyday Sweet and Spicy Pork Rub (see page 21)
1 tablespoon (11 g) mustard seeds
1 teaspoon dried thyme
1 teaspoon crushed red pepper flakes
½ teaspoon Old Bay Seasoning

2 tablespoons (30 g) light brown sugar, divided
3 tablespoons (45 ml) apple cider vinegar
2 tablespoons (28 ml) water
2 tablespoons (30 g) ketchup

METHOD

Prepare your smoker for a 300°F (150°C) 3 hour cook.

With a paper towel, peel the membrane off of the bone side of the ribs.

In a small bowl, combine the Everyday Sweet and Spicy Pork Rub, mustard seeds, dried thyme, red pepper flakes, Old Bay Seasoning, and 1 tablespoon (15 g) of brown sugar. Grind the mixture in your spice grinder to make a rub.

In a separate bowl, combine the vinegar, water, ketchup, and remaining 1 tablespoon (15 g) of brown sugar. Whisk thoroughly to make a mop sauce.

Using about 3 tablespoons (18 g) of rub per rack, dust the bone side of the ribs

with 1 tablespoon (6 g) of rub and then flip over and heavily dust the meat side, using the remaining 2 tablespoons (12 g). Place the ribs meat side up in your preheated smoker. Smoke for 45 minutes and then liberally mop. Mop the ribs every 30 minutes during cooking process until the mop is gone. Smoke the ribs until they have an internal temperature of 192 to 194°F (approximately 90°C) when measured in the thickest part of the meat between the bones, about 2½ to 3 hours. Another doneness cue is to pick up the ribs in the center with a pair of tongs; if the meat is just starting to pull away from the bone, the ribs are close to done.

When the ribs are done, remove from the smoker and let sit for 5 minutes before serving.

Liberally dust the racks with about 2 tablespoons (12 g) of rub on each rack right before you serve them.

STORAGE

Wrap room temperature leftover ribs tightly in plastic wrap. Refrigerate for up to 3 days or freeze for up to 1 month.

Wicked Good Chicken Rub

Prep time: 20 minutes
Yield: A little more than 1 cup (100 g)

INGREDIENTS

¼ cup (60 g) packed light brown sugar
¼ cup (50 g) granulated sugar
2 tablespoons (14 g) paprika
1 tablespoon (8 g) chili powder
1 tablespoon (6 g) ground black pepper
1 tablespoon (14 g) kosher salt
1 tablespoon (9 g) garlic powder
1 teaspoon crushed red pepper flakes
1 teaspoon dried thyme
1 teaspoon dried rosemary leaves

EQUIPMENT

Spice grinder

A barbecue chicken spice blend should be sweet and spicy with herbal background flavors that are complementary yet not overpowering. This one is perfect, especially on chicken wings tossed with some butter and hot sauce. It's important to process the finished rub in a spice grinder to ensure the flavors are well incorporated.

METHOD

Whisk the ingredients together in a mixing bowl. Working in batches if necessary, pulse the mixture in a spice grinder for 30 seconds to ensure even blending. Transfer to an airtight container.

STORAGE

Store in an airtight container out of the sunlight. Somewhere in the 1 to 2 month range the rub will start to lose its vibrant flavor.

Everyday Sweet and Spicy Pork Rub

Prep time: 20 minutes
Yield: Almost 3 ½ cups (350 g)

INGREDIENTS

1 cup (225 g) packed light brown sugar
½ cup (56 g) paprika
½ cup 112 g) kosher salt
½ cup (50 g) granulated sugar
3 tablespoons (24 g) chili powder
1 tablespoon (9 g) plus 2 teaspoons (6 g)
    garlic powder
1 tablespoon (7 g) plus 2 teaspoons (5 g)
    onion powder
2 tablespoons (14 g) ground cumin
2 tablespoons (12 g) ground black pepper
1 teaspoon ground cayenne pepper

This is a recipe we created in our early days of cooking barbecue before we got hot and heavy with competition. It's our good ol' standby; the one we suggest you use when winning the World Championship is not on the day's agenda. This rub is sweet and spicy, perfect for pork or chicken.

METHOD

Whisk all the ingredients together in a mixing bowl. Optionally, pulse the mixture in a spice grinder for 30 seconds to ensure maximum blending. Transfer to an airtight container.

STORAGE

Store in an airtight container out of the sunlight. Somewhere in the 1 to 2 month range the rub will start to lose its vibrant flavor.

Simple Beef Rub

Prep time: 15 minutes
Yield: Almost 2 ¼ cups (225 g)

INGREDIENTS

1 cup (96 g) coarse ground black pepper
1 cup (224 g) kosher salt
1 tablespoon (9 g) garlic powder
1 tablespoon (7 g) paprika

Hands down our two favorite items to smoke are beef short ribs and briskets. This rub, which is very similar to what Andy uses at The Smoke Shop, is a go-to for both of those cuts. It's also delicious on grilled steaks and pork chops. Try pushing the rub into the meat to get a great crust.

METHOD

In a bowl, combine all the ingredients and mix well.

STORAGE

Store in a tightly sealed container at room temperature out of direct sunlight. The rub will keep for a few months.

Juicy BBQ Chicken Breasts

Slow and low temperatures on a barbecue pit can easily dry out chicken breasts. At Andy's restaurant, Tremont 647, he discovered a few tricks to create perfectly juicy chicken: brining and cooking the chicken on the bone. It takes extra time, but it's worth it.

✴ BONUS: If you take fresh corn off the cob, blanch it, and toss it in the melted butter toward the end of your cooking process, you'll have one incredible side dish.

Prep time: 30 minutes, plus an overnight brine
Cook time: 2 hours
Serves: 4 as an entrée

INGREDIENTS

8 cups (1.9 L) water
5 tablespoons (70 g)
    plus ½ teaspoon kosher salt, divided
1 sprig of fresh thyme or
    ½ teaspoon dried thyme
1 sprig of fresh rosemary or
    ½ teaspoon dried rosemary leaves
1 teaspoon crushed red pepper flakes
1 teaspoon ground black pepper
4 bone-in split chicken breasts

8 tablespoons (112 g) salted butter, softened
¼ cup (15 g) parsley leaves, minced
1 clove of garlic, minced
1 tablespoon (15 ml) extra virgin olive oil
Zest of 1 lemon
3 tablespoons (18 g) Wicked Good Chicken
    Rub (see page 20) or your favorite rub,
    divided
½ cup (125 g) IQUE Sauce v2.0 (see page
    197) or your favorite barbecue sauce

METHOD

To make the brine: in a medium saucepan over high heat, combine the water and 5 tablespoons (70 g) of kosher salt. Bring to a simmer. Add the thyme, rosemary, red pepper flakes, and black pepper. Remove from the heat and cool to 40°F (5°C).

Rinse the chicken breasts in cold water and then submerge in the brine for 24 hours. Once the chicken is brined, remove and pat dry with a paper towel.

Preheat the smoker to 300°F (150°C) with apple or maple hardwood.

To make the butter: In a small bowl, combine the butter, garlic, olive oil, parsley, lemon zest, 1 tablespoon (6 g) of rub, and the remaining ½ teaspoon of kosher salt. Mix well.

Separate some of the skin from the chicken breast and slide the butter between the skin and the meat without ripping the skin. Use about 2 tablespoons (28 g) per breast.

Place the buttered chicken breasts in an ovenproof baking dish with any leftover butter. Dust the chicken skin with the remaining 2 tablespoons (12 g) of rub.

Place the pan in your preheated smoker. Every 20 minutes, use a spoon to baste the chicken with the melted butter on the bottom of the pan.

Meanwhile, in a saucepan over low heat, start to warm the barbecue sauce.

Once the chicken has hit an internal temperature of 140°F (60°C)—about 45 minutes—brush the chicken with the hot barbecue sauce. Continue to cook to an internal temperature of 158°F (70°C). Remove the pan from the smoker and set the chicken breast on a rack to rest for 5 to 10 minutes before serving.

The remaining butter in the pan can be used on corn, peas, or mashed potatoes or even as a dipping sauce for some toasted French bread.

STORAGE

Wrap room temperature leftover chicken tightly in plastic wrap. Refrigerate for up to 3 days or freeze for up to 1 month.

Classic Pulled Pork on a Kamado–style Ceramic Smoker

We've both owned dozens of smokers over the years. Most of them come and go, but a kamado–style ceramic smoker (such as the Big Green Egg) is a keeper for both its versatility and its excellent insulation. It keeps us smoking all winter in New England.

Once you've got the right equipment, you need to get the timing down. A common mistake we see with new barbecue cooks is underestimating how long things will take. If you are cooking only for yourself, you don't have to worry so much. But if eight hungry friends are waiting on your pork shoulder, it can be a problem. Plan instead to have the meat done two hours before you want to eat and keep it warm in a cooler until meal time.

We've used this recipe as an opportunity to delve into the specifics of operating a kamado–style ceramic smoker. However, this recipe can be adapted to any type of smoker by utilizing the same basic principles.

Prep time: 4 hours, with 1 hour active time
Cook time: About 10 to 12 hours, mostly unattended
Serves: 8 to 10

INGREDIENTS

1 bone-in Boston butt pork shoulder (8 to 10 pounds, or 3.6 to 4.6 kg)
⅓ cup (33 g) Everyday Sweet and Spicy Pork Rub, plus extra rub for serving (see page 21)
1 cup (250 g) Gold Sauce (see page 47) or your favorite barbecue sauce, warmed

SPECIAL EQUIPMENT

Kamado–style smoker
Lump charcoal
Charcoal chimney
Plate setter
2 chunks of wood about the size of a baseball (Apple, Cherry, and Oak are solid choices.)
Probe thermometer and ½ of an onion

METHOD

To prepare the smoker: Fill the smoker ¾ full with unlit charcoal and the two chunks of wood. This will seem like more charcoal than you need, but the smoker operates best with a full load of charcoal. Fill the charcoal chimney ¾ full and light two sheets of crumpled newspaper in the base. Once the charcoal is lit (the flames should just start to peak through the top of the charcoal), pour the lit charcoal into the smoker. Insert the plate setter, legs up, and then place the cooking grate on top. Cut an onion in half and push the probe thermometer through one half. Place the onion half cut side down on the grate. Open the lower vent about 3 inches (7.5 cm). Adjust the daisy wheel exhaust on top of the smoker so that the sliding section is closed and the rotating section is completely open.

If you are cooking overnight (about 12 hours), the target temperature is 225°F (110°C). If you are cooking during the day (about 8 hours), the target temperature is 275°F (135°C). Close the lower vent and the daisy wheel exhaust gradually to maintain the target temperature. Typically, you can maintain 225°F (110°C) with the lower vent open ½ inch (1.3 cm) and the daisy wheel exhaust open 25 percent. For 275°F (135°C), the lower vent is open 1 inch (2.5 cm) and the daisy wheel exhaust is open 50 percent. However, this will vary depending on factors like lump charcoal density and the weather. The goal is to maintain a steady temperature for at least one hour before adding the pork. Running about 25°F (5°C) above your target is fine; when the cold pork goes on the smoker, the temperature will naturally decrease.

While the smoker is heating, prepare the pork shoulder.

OVERNIGHT TIMELINE AT 225°F (110°C)

8 p.m.	Light the smoker.
9 p.m.	Prep the pork shoulder.
10 p.m.	The pork shoulder goes into the smoker fat side up.
12 a.m.	Optional check in (recommended for first time)
3 a.m.	Optional check in (recommended for first time)
7 a.m.	Flip the pork shoulder fat side down. Check the internal temperature. If the internal temperature is less than 175°F (80°C), increase the smoker temperature to 275°F (135°C) by opening the lower vents and exhaust.
8 to 10 a.m.	Check the internal temperature hourly until it reaches 200°F (95°C).

DAYTIME TIMELINE AT 275°F (135°C)

6 a.m.	Light the smoker.
7 a.m.	Prep the pork shoulder.
8 a.m.	The pork shoulder goes into the smoker fat side up
2 p.m.	Flip the pork shoulder fat side down. Check the internal temperature. If the internal temperature is less than 175°F (80°C), increase the smoker temperature to 300°F (150°C) by opening the lower vents and exhaust.
3 to 6 p.m.	Check the internal temperature hourly until it reaches 200°F (95°C)

Remove the pork shoulder from the fridge and place in the sink. Cut away the packaging and rinse the shoulder with cold water. Move the shoulder to a large piece of aluminum foil. Dry with a paper towel and sprinkle liberally with Everyday Sweet and Spicy Pork Rub. Pat the rub into the shoulder with your hands. Let the shoulder sit at room temperature until the smoker is ready. Build an oval-shaped drip pan with three large pieces of aluminum foil. Crinkle up the edges until the aluminum foil "pan" will just fit into the dimensions of the plate setter.

Once the smoker has been running rock solid for at least an hour, it's time to cook. Remove the cooking grate and with tongs or gloved hands push the plate setter up a bit and drop in the two chunks of wood. Place the aluminum foil drip pan on the plate setter. Return the cooking grate to the smoker. Place the pork shoulder on the grate fat side up. Position the probe thermometer onion setup so it is above the drip pan but not touching the pork. Close the lid. Reopen the lid and double check that the positioning of the probe is correct.

Okay, now it's time to kick back and relax. The basic instructions for overnight or daytime cooking schedules are above.

Once the internal temperature reaches 200°F (95°C), the pork shoulder is done.

To hold the pork until serving, wrap it tightly in aluminum foil. Pour some hot tap water into a small cooler. Close the cooler for 10 minutes. Remove the water, place the pork shoulder into the cooler, and close the lid. A 2 to 4 hour hold is ideal, but you can push it to as long as 6 hours as long as the internal temperature of the meat doesn't fall below 140°F (60°C).

To serve, place the pork shoulder in a serving pan. Remove the bone. Using tongs and a fork, shred the pork into large chunks. For a finer product, move the pork in batches to a cutting board and chop with a knife. Mix the pork with the sauce. Season with some extra Everyday Sweet and Spicy Pork Rub and serve. The classic pairing is potato buns and slaw.

STORAGE
Wrap room temperature leftover pork tightly in plastic wrap. Refrigerate for up to 3 days or freeze for up to 1 month.

Drink
—LOCAL—

Barbecue and beer are clearly in the food and beverage pairing hall of fame.

Just as there are diverse regions and styles of barbecue, there are even more options in the world of beer: A cold can of American pilsner is a fantastic palate cleanser as you work your way through a plate of Memphis-style ribs.

But we are also interested in beers that accentuate the smoky, caramelized, spicy nature of American barbecue. One unexpectedly great match for barbecue is a bittersweet coffee stout that will intensify the spice and the richness of the meat. Porters and malt-forward brown ales are also excellent choices.

Regardless of the style you prefer, perhaps the best pairings are the offerings from your local brewer. Nothing beats picking up a beer straight from the brewery that is fresh and served exactly as the brewer intended.

Next time you spend all weekend creating perfect barbecue, pair it up with beer from a local brewer that is brimming with that same love of craft.

Beef Barbecue

If you haven't added a smoker to your arsenal yet, this is a great recipe to try two-zone–style cooking on your charcoal or gas grill (see page 15 for detailed instructions). The chuck cut of beef holds up really well to a bit of direct heat and assertive smoke flavor. We like hickory best.

Prep time: 15 minutes
Cook time: 4 to 5 hours
Serves: 6 to 8

INGREDIENTS

1 beef chuck roast or beef brisket flat
  (6 to 8 pounds, or 2.7 to 3.6 kg)
2 tablespoons (22 g) yellow mustard
¼ cup (25 g) Simple Beef Rub (see page 21)
½ cup (120 g) of the beer you are drinking
  (Hop forward beers can turn bitter during
  the cooking process. A dark malty beer such
  as stout or porter is an excellent choice.)
½ cup (125 g) Kansas City Tribute Sauce,
  warmed (see page 93)

METHOD

Trim the beef of excess fat and brush all sides with yellow mustard. Sprinkle the beef with the Simple Beef Rub.

Prepare your smoker for a 325°F (170°C) 4 to 5 hour cook or preheat a grill to 325°F (170°) and adjust for indirect cooking.

Place the beef on the smoker or grill, close the lid, and then no peeking for the next 2 hours. After 2 hours, flip the beef and cook for an additional hour. Transfer the beef onto two large sheets of aluminum foil. Pour the beer over the beef. Tightly wrap the beef in the aluminum foil and return to the smoker or grill until a meat thermometer inserted reads 200°F (95°C), about 1 additional hour.

Remove the wrapped beef from the smoker or grill and let rest for 30 minutes. Remove the beef from the aluminum foil and place on a cutting board. Save the drippings. Slice or pull the beef. In a serving bowl, mix the beef with the reserved drippings and warm Kansas City Tribute Sauce. Serve immediately.

STORAGE

Wrap room temperature beef tightly in plastic wrap. Refrigerate up to 3 days or freeze up to 1 month.

The BBQ Glaze

You can make this glaze with maple syrup, cane syrup, honey, sorghum, or molasses depending on what you are cooking. We also like to add roasted spicy hot peppers to the mix. About a tablespoon (11 g) of minced charred peppers will give your sauce a unique—and hot—flavor. Jalapeños to habaneros, choose the spiciness you like.

Prep Time: 5 minutes
Cook time: 20 minutes
Yield: 5 cups (1.3 kg)

INGREDIENTS

1 cup (22g) packed light brown sugar
1 cup (340 g) honey or (235 ml) maple syrup
½ cup (120 ml) apple cider vinegar
1 teaspoon mustard seeds
1 teaspoon dried thyme
1 teaspoon minced garlic
1 teaspoon garlic powder
1 teaspoon ground black pepper

1 teaspoon crushed red pepper flakes
1 teaspoon cumin seeds, toasted and ground
1 teaspoon kosher salt
2 cups (480 g) ketchup
2 tablespoons (22 g) yellow mustard
2 tablespoons (28 ml) Worcestershire sauce
2 teaspoons Fermented Chili Sauce
  (see page 62) or your favorite hot sauce

METHOD

Combine the brown sugar, honey or maple syrup, vinegar, and spices in a small saucepan over medium high heat. Bring to a boil, stirring occasionally, and then lower the heat to medium and simmer for 4 minutes.

Add the ketchup, mustard, Worcestershire sauce, and Fermented Chili Sauce and mix well. Simmer, stirring occasionally, for 5 minutes more.

Cool to room temperature and pour off into three pint-sized (475 ml) Mason jars.

STORAGE

Refrigerate, tightly covered, for up to 2 months.

"Barbecue Is My Life"

by Ken "Jake" Jacobs

BOSTON BARBECUE LEGEND

The first time I saw a Texas pitmaster take a brisket out of the smoker, it was all black. I thought it was a joke. I thought, "This is a burnt piece of meat. I can't eat that." Well, the guys sliced it, and the juice was running out of it. He gave me a piece to try. It was the most fascinating piece of meat that I've ever tasted. That's where this all started.

Not a lot of people were barbecuing in Boston then. No one could believe I was cooking with wood and not charcoal or gas.

I was 11 years old the first time my uncle let me man the grill at a family cookout. It became a hobby for me. I cooked outside every Sunday in the cold, the snow, whatever. But it wasn't until I moved from New England to Texas that I realized that what I was doing all those years wasn't barbecue. That was grilling. This was barbecue.

I started to learn the Texas barbecue traditions from someone who had been cooking for a long time. I wanted to cook brisket right away, but he kept putting me off. He started me out cooking pork shoulder. I would sit there for hours cooking pork shoulder. When I finally got that right, he let me cook a brisket.

I moved back to Boston in the 1980s and I brought my smoker with me. When I was a kid in Boston in the '60s, there was a guy from my neighborhood—Jimmy, he's the sort of guy you don't forget—who set up his smokers on the street on Friday and Saturday nights. People would line up for that barbecue. So I set up my smokers on Blue Hill Avenue in Dorchester and I started to attract a crowd. Not a lot of people were barbecuing in Boston then. No one could believe I was cooking with wood and not charcoal or gas.

Not long after, I entered a competition in Cleveland. It was our first time out and we took third place. We started to get attention for our style of barbecue. It's a little different: I think of myself as a "smokemaster" more than a pitmaster. I'm fascinated by finding ways to infuse flavor through the smoke. I just smell smoke from a grill and I'm headed in that direction.

I cooked in Texas and I cooked in Boston—we'd start at two in the afternoon and be out there until late, late at night—and I cooked in Georgia. Now, I still cater parties sometimes. Barbecue is my life. If I woke up one day and I couldn't go and light up a smoker, it would drive me crazy.

Jake's Cowboy Beans

This is one of Jake's bread and butter recipes. These beans were inspired by Texas barbecue tradition, but he served them late night on the streets of Boston. It's hard to go wrong with a base of flavors that include cane syrup, coffee, bourbon, and barbecue brisket.

Prep time: Overnight
Cook time: 2 hours
Serves: 6 to 8 as a side dish

INGREDIENTS

2 cups (about 1 pound, or 455 g)
  dry pinto beans
2 cup (500 g) barbecue sauce such
  as Red State Sauce (see page 129)
1 cup (320 g) cane syrup
1 cup (235 ml) brewed coffee
½ cup (120 ml) bourbon
1 pound (455 g) chopped barbecue brisket

4 tablespoons (30 g) chili powder
2 tablespoons (14 g) ground cumin
2 tablespoons (8 g) red pepper flakes
Kosher salt, to taste

METHOD

Soak the pinto beans overnight in cold water. Strain the beans and place in a 6-quart (5.7 L) saucepan. Cover the beans with water and bring to a simmer over medium heat. Cook uncovered, stirring occasionally, until just tender, about 1 hour. Drain the beans and return to the saucepan. Add the barbecue sauce, cane syrup, coffee, bourbon, chopped brisket, chili powder, cumin, and red pepper flakes. Simmer for 30 minutes. Taste and add kosher salt as needed.

STORAGE

Refrigerate in an airtight container for up to 1 week.

Cornbread with Butter, Honey, and Sea Salt

This is the cornbread served at The Smoke Shop. There are many schools of thought on what makes cornbread traditional Southern cornbread: sugar vs. no sugar, flour vs. no flour. Luckily, we aren't making any claims that this is a traditional Southern cornbread. In fact, it's just the opposite. It's what we grew up with in New England: cakey, light, a bit sweet, and craveable. But it's best to not say how much butter you've used.

CORNBREAD
Prep time: 15 minutes
Cook time: 1 hour
Yield: About 24 small pieces

CORNBREAD INGREDIENTS
2 cups (400 g) granulated sugar, divided
3½ cups (438 g) all purpose flour
2½ cups (350 g) coarse yellow cornmeal
1 teaspoon table salt
2 tablespoons (9 g) baking powder
4 large eggs
1½ cups (355 ml) whole milk
1½ cups (355 ml) buttermilk
2½ tablespoons (38 ml) vegetable oil
½ cup (120 ml) melted butter
1 batch of Honey Sea Salt Butter, softened

HONEY SEA SALT BUTTER INGREDIENTS
1 cup (225 g) salted butter, softened
¼ cup (85 g) wildflower honey
½ teaspoon kosher salt
1 teaspoon large flake sea salt, such as Maldon Sea Salt

CORNBREAD METHOD

Preheat the oven to 350°F (180°C, or gas mark 4). Coat a 13 x 9-inch (33 x 23 cm) baking pan with cooking spray and dust with 1 cup (200 g) of granulated sugar.

Sift together the flour, cornmeal, remaining 1 cup (200 g) of sugar, salt, and baking powder.

In the bowl of a stand mixer fitted with a whisk attachment, combine the eggs, milks, oil, and melted butter. Mix on low for 2 minutes until combined. Turn off the mixer and add the dry ingredients in three batches, whipping on low after each addition until combined.

After all of the dry ingredients have been added, use a rubber spatula to scrape the bottom of the bowl and combine any remaining ingredients into the batter. Whip the batter on medium for 5 minutes.

Pour the batter into the center of the pan and let it spread naturally to the sides of the baking pan. Bake for 45 minutes to 1 hour until a toothpick inserted in the center of the bread comes out clean. It should be lightly golden brown on top.

Place on a cooling rack and cool 10 minutes before cutting into 24 pieces. Spread softened Honey Sea Salt Butter over the corn bread pieces and serve warm.

HONEY SEA SALT BUTTER METHOD

Place the butter, honey, and kosher salt in small stainless steel bowl and mix well with a rubber spatula or wooden spoon until fully incorporated. Fold in the sea salt.

STORAGE

Wrap tightly and refrigerate for up to 2 weeks.

Classic Macaroni and Cheese

We grew up on Kraft macaroni and cheese. Homemade stovetop macaroni and cheese is almost as simple to make: Make your sauce, cook your macaroni, mix, and serve.

Prep time: 15 minutes
Cook time: 20 minutes
Serves: 6 to 8

INGREDIENTS

1 pound (455 g) elbow macaroni
2 cups (475 ml) whole milk
¼ cup (60 ml) water
4 tablespoons (55 g) unsalted butter, divided
3 tablespoons (24 g) all purpose flour
Tiny pinch of ground nutmeg
¼ teaspoon ground white pepper
1 teaspoon kosher salt
2 cups (450 g) shredded yellow Cheddar cheese
¼ cup (40 g) shredded Parmesan cheese

METHOD

Cook the elbow macaroni according to package instructions until al dente. When the pasta is done, strain well, place back in pan, and mix with 1 tablespoon (14 g) of butter.

While the pasta cooks, prepare the cheese sauce.

In a bowl, combine the milk and water.

In a medium, heavy-bottom saucepan over low heat, melt the remaining 3 tablespoons (45 g) of butter. Add the flour and stir with a fork continually until the mixture (roux) is well combined and has a nutty aroma, about 2 to 3 minutes. The roux should not brown. Slowly add the milk mixture to the roux, whisking until fully incorporated. Add the nutmeg, white pepper, and kosher salt. Increase the heat to medium-high to bring the mixture to a simmer, whisking frequently as it heats. Simmer the mixture, stirring occasionally with a wooden spoon to prevent scorching, until it is a little thicker than maple syrup and coats the back of the spoon, about 5 minutes. Remove the sauce from the heat. Fold in the cheeses and stir well. Add the macaroni and taste for seasoning, adding kosher salt and pepper as needed. Serve hot.

STORAGE

Refrigerate in an airtight container for up to 3 days.

"A Golden Age of Barbecue"

by Steven Raichlen

BARBECUE AUTHOR AND TELEVISION HOST

Last year, I was inducted into the Barbecue Hall of Fame in Kansas City. It was one of those "pinch me" moments. I thought: "How did I get here? How did this happen?" And yet, when I reflect on my life and on the evolution of barbecue in the United States, it all makes perfect sense.

I probably have the weirdest background in barbecue: Growing up in Baltimore, the closest thing to barbecue I ever had was Chinese carry-out ribs on Sunday night. I got a degree in French literature, and when I graduated from college, I was offered a Fulbright to study paleography, the science of ancient handwriting. Instead, I took a Watson Foundation fellowship to study medieval cooking in Europe. That got me thinking about the inter-section of food and history and culture, which is what I've been doing ever since in my cookbooks.

I've written about many different topics, but when I hit on barbecue, it was one of those light bulb moments: Grilling is one of the oldest and most universal cooking methods in the world. Virtually every culture does it, but every culture does it in a different way. So I thought, "Wouldn't it be cool to travel around the world and docu-ment how people barbecue in different countries?" That eventually became *The Barbecue! Bible*. I thought it was going to be a modest book, but it grew into this 600-page monster that took me four years to write. It came out at exactly the right time.

When I started in barbecue around 1994, Americans grilled mostly on special occasions and it was usually hot dogs, hamburgers, and steaks. There was a complete ignorance of global grilling and few people even knew what indirect grilling was. But now the outdoor kitchen has become an extension of the indoor kitchen. We grill five nights a week and 32 percent of American families own more than one grill. And once you've mastered

> *In an increasingly homogenized world, [barbecue is] some of the last truly regional food we have.*

your grill, the next step is barbecue. People are smoking things in their back-yard in ways that you would have once only found in barbecue restaurants.

It's the perfect storm. You've got people who are ready to go beyond the grill and you've got all this celebration of barbecue. There are TV shows like *BBQ Pitmasters* and my *Primal Grill* and *Project Smoke*, and the incredible publicity

around pitmasters like Aaron Franklin. I mean, he won a James Beard Foundation Award in a category historically reserved for fine dining. Plus, the grill and smoker industry has introduced a whole new set of tools that are affordable, easy to use, and small enough to fit into your backyard. All those things have come together to usher in a golden age of barbecue.

So much is happening right now that I am excited about. People are starting to talk about where their meat comes from; there's more interest in quality. And we've seen the globalization in grilling—which was my goal in books like *Planet Barbecue!* and *The Barbecue! Bible*—extend into smoking. But I will say that one of the things I still love and cherish about barbecue is that in an increasingly homogenized world, it's some of the last truly regional food we have. I celebrate that and hope we never lose it.

Caveman T-Bones with Hellfire Hot Sauce

It's hard to imagine something more primal than grilling meat over fire. But Steven Raichlen goes next level in his book *Planet Barbecue!* with the "cavemanning" method: steak cooked directly on the embers for a wonderful crust and smoky flavor.

Cook time: 10 minutes
Yield: 2 big steaks; serves 2 to 4

INGREDIENTS

2 T-bone steaks (each 12 to 14 ounces [340 to 395 g] and 2-inches [5 cm] thick)
Coarse salt (kosher or sea) and coarsely cracked black peppercorns

FOR THE HELLFIRE HOT SAUCE:

½ cup (120 ml) extra virgin olive oil
10 jalapeño peppers, thinly sliced crosswise
10 cloves of garlic, thinly sliced
¾ cup (12 g) loosely packed cilantro leaves, coarsely chopped

SPECIAL EQUIPMENT

12-inch (30 cm) cast iron pan

METHOD

Grill the steaks: Build a charcoal fire—natural lump charcoal, please—and rake the coals into an even layer. (Leave the front third of your grill coal-free; this is a safety zone.) When the coals glow orange, fan them with a newspaper to blow off any loose ash.

Generously, and I mean generously, season the steaks on both sides with salt and cracked pepper. Place the steaks directly on the embers about 2 inches (5 cm) apart. Grill until cooked to taste, about 4 minutes per side for medium-rare, turning with tongs. Move the steaks after 2 minutes on each side so they cook evenly. Use the "poke" test to check for doneness.

Using tongs, lift the steaks out of the fire, shaking each to dislodge any clinging embers. Using a basting brush, brush off any loose ash and arrange the steaks on a platter or plates. Cover loosely with aluminum foil. Let the steaks rest for 2 minutes while you make the Hellfire Hot Sauce.

Heat the olive oil in a cast iron skillet directly on the embers, on the side burner of a gas grill, or on the stove. When the oil is hot, add the jalapeños and garlic. Cook over high heat until the jalapeños and garlic begin to brown, about 2 minutes. Stir in the cilantro. Pour the Hellfire Hot Sauce over the steaks and serve.

STORAGE

Wrap room temperature steak tightly in plastic wrap. Refrigerate up to 3 days.

Recipe by Steve Raichlin; used with permission.

Smoked Bologna Chub

Just like playing music or brewing beer, the key to cooking great barbecue is repetition. If you are just getting started with barbecue, you will ruin some meat before you get it right. This smoked bologna recipe is a delicious and very cheap way to get in those reps without worrying about destroying an expensive piece of meat.

Prep time: 20 minutes
Cook time: 4 hours
Serves: 10 to 12 as part of a barbecue meal

INGREDIENTS

1 skinless bologna chub (5 pounds, or 2.3 kg)
⅓ cup (58 g) yellow mustard
2 tablespoons (12 g) Everyday Sweet and Spicy Pork Rub (see page 21)
1 tablespoon (12 g) turbinado sugar
20 to 24 pieces (2 per guest) of Texas Toast (see page 141)
½ of a large sweet onion, thinly sliced
1 cup (119 g) bread and butter pickles
1 cup (250 g) of your favorite barbecue sauce, warmed

METHOD

If the bologna has a skin, remove it. Score the bologna with 6 evenly spaced, horizontal cuts about ½-inch (1.3 cm) deep and then repeat with 6 evenly spaced vertical cuts, creating a crisscross pattern. Place the bologna on a sheet pan and brush the exterior with yellow mustard. Sprinkle on the Everyday Sweet and Spicy Pork Rub and refrigerate for at least 1 hour or overnight.

Prepare your smoker for a 235°F (115°C) 3 to 4 hour cook.

The bologna is already cooked and will pick up just a touch of smoke flavor, so use a fairly heavy hand on the smoke wood. For example, add at least 3 fist-sized chunks of hickory wood to a charcoal base in your WSM or cabinet smoker. Sprinkle the exterior with the turbinado sugar and place the bologna on your clean grill grate. Smoke for three hours. Keep your temps pinned at 235 to 250°F (115 to 120°C). After

three hours, a crusty bark should have formed on the exterior. If the crust is not quite to your liking, cook the bologna for another hour. Remove the bologna and let it rest for 15 minutes.

Prepare two pieces of Texas Toast per guest. Slice the bologna into ½-inch (1.3 cm) slices. Serve with the toast, thinly sliced onions, pickles, and barbecue sauce.

STORAGE

Wrap room temperature bologna tightly in plastic wrap. Refrigerate for up to 3 days or freeze up to 1 month.

Spicy Collards

In our book *Wicked Good Barbecue*, we featured a classic stewed collards recipe. Here, we have an unconventional preparation of a classic barbecue side dish. The results are light, refreshing, and spicy—the perfect foil to rich barbecue meats.

Prep time: 10 minutes
Cook time: 10 minutes
Serves: 6 to 8 as a side dish

INGREDIENTS

2 tablespoons (28 ml) extra virgin olive oil
1 tablespoon (10 g) minced garlic
2 teaspoon crushed red pepper flakes
1 teaspoon kosher salt, plus more for seasoning
2 bunches of collard greens, stems removed and
  leaves cut into ⅛-inch (3 mm) ribbons

METHOD

In a large, heavy-bottomed sauté pan over medium high heat, heat the oil. Add the garlic, crushed red pepper flakes, and kosher salt. Stir continuously until garlic starts to brown, about 1 to 2 minutes. Add the collard greens. Use tongs to stir and toss the collard greens, coating with the oil and seasoning, until wilted, about 3 to 4 minutes. Remove from the heat and taste for seasoning; a little more kosher salt might be needed. Serve immediately.

STORAGE

Refrigerate for up to 3 days.

Gold Sauce

Gold Sauce utilizes mustard as a base instead of the typical ketchup. Often found in South Carolina, the sauce provides the tang found in North Carolina vinegar sauces, yet with the texture and consistency of a classic Kansas City–type sauce. This is our favorite all around sauce and pairs well not only with classic barbecue but pork chops, hot dogs, and even as a potato chip dip.

Cook time: 20 minutes
Yield: 3 cups (750 g)

INGREDIENTS

½ cup (120 ml) apple cider vinegar
¼ cup (60 ml) water
2 tablespoons (40 g) blackstrap molasses
¾ cup (255 g) honey
1 tablespoon (15 ml) maple syrup
1 teaspoon dried thyme
½ teaspoon ground white pepper

Pinch ground nutmeg
1 cup (176 g) yellow mustard
½ teaspoon kosher salt
½ cup (80 g) grated yellow onion
1 teaspoon crushed red pepper flakes

METHOD

Combine the honey, vinegar, water, molasses, maple syrup, thyme, white pepper, and nutmeg in a small saucepan over medium-high heat. Bring to a boil, stirring continuously. Reduce the heat to medium and simmer gently for 4 minutes, stirring occasionally.

Add the mustard and kosher salt, mix well, and simmer for 1 minute more. Remove from the heat and add the onion and red pepper flakes, if using. Serve hot or cold.

STORAGE

Refrigerate in a pint-sized (475 ml) Mason jar for up to 2 months.

Garlicky Coleslaw

Most dishes benefit from roasted garlic and coleslaw is no exception. Hit up your next pulled pork sandwich with a few spoonfuls of this creamy, tangy, savory rendition. For the best results, make the slaw the day before you plan to eat it and let the flavors meld overnight in the fridge.

Prep time: 2 hours with at least 4 hours rest time
Serves: 8 to 10 as a side dish

INGREDIENTS
1 head of garlic
1 cup (225 g) prepared mayonnaise (ideally Duke's Mayonnaise)
⅓ cup (80 ml) apple cider vinegar
⅓ cup (100 g) granulated sugar
1 tablespoon (11 g) yellow mustard
1 teaspoon table salt
1 teaspoon ground black pepper
1 tablespoon (15 ml) fresh lemon juice
1 pound (455 g) packaged dry coleslaw mix
2 teaspoons barbecue dry rub

METHOD
Preheat the oven—Chris uses his toaster oven—to 300°F (150°C, or gas mark 2). Wrap the garlic in aluminum foil and place in the oven. Cook for 1 hour. Turn off the oven and let the garlic sit in the oven for 30 minutes. Remove and cool. Cut the garlic head in half with a serrated knife. Press down on the garlic to extract the roasted cloves. Process the cloves into a paste with the side of your knife. Put the roasted garlic in a blender along with the mayonnaise, vinegar, sugar, and mustard. Pulse until well combined, about 30 seconds. Add the salt and pepper and lemon juice. Pulse the blender for 5 seconds.

Place the coleslaw mix in a large bowl and add the dressing. Mix well. The slaw at this stage may seem a bit dry. Refrigerate at least 4 hours and ideally overnight. The time in the fridge will meld the flavors and kick up moisture as the salt draws some liquid from the cabbage. Before serving, sprinkle with the barbecue dry rub.

STORAGE
Refrigerate in a covered container for up to 3 days.

Old-Fashioned Southern Caramel Cake

Andy's dear friend Mark Ballard, a *bon vivant* from Macon, Georgia, learned how to make this cake from his grandmother when he wasn't even tall enough to reach the stove top. While you finish icing the cake, have someone you love set out the knife, plates, forks, and the milk or coffee. Eat the cake warm for an absolutely wonderful sugar coma. We think this classic Southern dessert is the perfect finale to a barbecue meal.

Prep time: 1 hour
Cook time: 1 hour
Serves: 12 to 14

INGREDIENTS

1 cup (225 g) unsalted butter,
    room temperature
3 cups (600 g) granulated sugar
6 large eggs
1 cup (230 g) sour cream
1 teaspoon vanilla extract
2⅔ cups (341 g) cake flour
1 teaspoon table salt
¼ teaspoon baking soda
1 batch of Southern Caramel Icing

METHOD

Preheat the oven to 350°F (180°, or gas mark 4). Coat an 18 x 13-inch (46 x 33 cm) sheet pan with cooking spray and dust it with flour, knocking out any excess.

In the bowl of a stand mixer fitted with a paddle attachment, cream the butter, adding sugar gradually until the butter is light and fluffy. Add the eggs one at a time, blending well after each. Add the sour cream and vanilla and mix well. Add the cake flour, salt, and baking soda, blending until fully combined. Spread the batter evenly in the prepared pan and bake until a toothpick inserted in the center of the cake comes out clean, about 15 to 20 minutes. Do not overbake. Cool the cake in its pan on a rack while you prepare the icing.

When the icing is ready, immediately pour it over the cake, spreading it quickly with a large offset spatula before it sets. (It's fine if the cake is still warm; the icing will set as it cools.) Slice and serve warm with coffee or an ice-cold glass of milk.

STORAGE

Wrap in plastic wrap and refrigerate for up to 3 days.

SOUTHERN CARAMEL ICING

Caramel icing is notoriously tricky to get right. Some Southerners say it takes years of practice. The key is to pay close attention to the temperature as the icing cooks and whisk it constantly as it cools. Otherwise, it will become grainy. If the icing gets too cool to spread, it can be remelted over low heat. Whip it again to spreading consistency.

Cook time: 30 minutes
Yield: 2 cups (450 g)

INGREDIENTS

3½ cups (700 g) granulated sugar, divided
½ cup (120 ml) boiling water
1 cup (235 ml) evaporated milk
½ cup (112 g) unsalted butter
1 tablespoon (22 g) light corn syrup
1 teaspoon vanilla extract

SPECIAL EQUIPMENT

Candy thermometer

METHOD

In a small, heavy saucepan or skillet, cook ½ cup (100 g) of sugar over medium-low heat until melted and caramelized. Carefully pour boiling water into the pan and boil, stirring, until the caramel dissolves and the mixture is slightly syrupy, about 5 minutes.

In another saucepan, combine the remaining 3 cups (600 g) of sugar, evaporated milk, butter, and corn syrup over medium heat, stirring to melt the sugar. Attach a candy thermometer to the pan and bring to a boil, stirring occasionally. Add the caramel syrup and continue to cook, stirring, until the mixture reaches 218 to 220°F (approximately 105°C). Remove the pan from the heat and immediately transfer the mixture to a stand mixer fitted with a whisk attachment. Beat the icing until it cools and thickens just enough to hold its shape when the whisk is lifted. The icing should still be very warm and soft, pourable but not runny. Use immediately.

NOTE: Hitting the proper cooking temperature results in the best icing. If you aren't sure, put a spoonful of icing on a cold plate. It should set up quickly, soft but not sticky or hard. If it is still sticky after a couple of minutes, return the icing to the saucepan, simmer for just a few minutes, and then do the "plate test" again. If the icing hardened on the plate test, it's overcooked but you still may be able to save it: return the icing to the pan, whisk in a few tablespoons (45 to 60 ml) of heavy cream, bring it to a simmer, and test it again.

North Carolina

"The pig. A wonderful, magical animal."

–HOMER SIMPSON

No other barbecue region has the singular focus of North Carolina. We were first introduced to North Carolina barbecue on a pit stop while driving to Lynchburg, Tennessee, for the Jack Daniels World Championship in 2002. Northern guys like us were used to barbecue restaurants that covered all of the bases —ribs, beef, chicken, Texas style, Memphis style, and everything in between. In North Carolina, we found there is only one thing that matters—pork barbecue.

Limited side dishes provide an opportunity to add hushpuppies and vinegar slaw to your tray. Some joints offer fine chop, coarse chop, or sliced variations on the pork shoulder. Regional differences—barely perceptible to an outsider—include whole hog with chopped crispy skin and vinegar sauce to the East and whole shoulder with a touch of ketchup added to the vinegar sauce to the West. In order to appreciate the delicious simplicity of North Carolina barbecue, you have to slow down, pour a second glass of sweet tea, and bask in the glory created by the basic ingredients of pork, salt, vinegar, and hickory smoke. If there is anything in this world that proves that the sum can be greater than its parts, it is a plate of North Carolina pork barbecue.

Why pork? We'll go with the simplest answer: There are lots of pigs in North Carolina. There's also lots of hickory wood and a population of barbecue-loving folks who share the philosophy, "If the wheel ain't broke, why fix it?" The uniquely North Carolina method of pork, simply salted and cooked directly over hickory burned to coals, is incredibly primal and creates a wonderful sense of place. That is the power of barbecue.

In this chapter, we offer classic North Carolina barbecue recipes that can be cooked anywhere. So go ahead, whip yourself up a Western North Carolina–style shoulder, some hushpuppies fried in lard, and a big glass of sweet tea. If you close your eyes, you may just be whisked away to pork barbecue country.

Western North Carolina Pork Shoulder on a Weber Smokey Mountain Cooker

In Western North Carolina barbecue restaurants, you usually have three options for pork shoulder: coarsely chopped "outside brown," finely chopped inner meat, and sliced meat. When he makes this at home, Chris likes to serve all three. He also crisps the pig skin in lard. You can incorporate the crispy skin into the chopped meat or make your guests some classic Pork Skin Sandwiches (see page 57) as an appetizer.

This recipe can be adapted to any type of smoker. The key here is not the type of smoker, but creating a dry, hot 300 to 325°F (150 to 160°C) cooking environment.

✳ NOTE: In North Carolina, burn barrels are used to create coals. You can use that method here, but lump charcoal produces similar results in this recipe.

Prep time: 1 hour
Cook time: 10 to 12 hours
Serves: 10 to 12

INGREDIENTS
1 bone-in skin-on pork picnic shoulder
    (8 to 10 pounds, or 3.6 to 4.6 kg)
About ¾ cup (168 g) kosher salt
1 cup (205 g) lard or (235 ml) vegetable oil
About ¼ cup (60 ml) Western-Style
    North Carolina Sauce (see page 74)

SPECIAL EQUIPMENT
18-or 22½-inch (46 to 57 cm) Weber Smokey
    Mountain Cooker
High-quality lump charcoal
Charcoal chimney
3 fist-sized dry chunks of hickory and/or oak
12-inch (30 cm) cast iron pan

METHOD

Rub a heavy coating of kosher salt over the entire exterior of the pork shoulder. Let sit at room temperature for 1 hour while you prepare your smoker.

Start by filling the charcoal ring to the brim with lump charcoal and then line the water pan with aluminum foil. Fill a charcoal chimney ¾ full with lump charcoal and fill the base with two sheets of crumpled newspaper.

Place the chimney on top of the unlit charcoal and light the newspaper. When the charcoal is lit and flames are starting to peak out, pour the lit charcoal on top of the unlit. Assemble your Weber

Smokey Mountain Cooker with the water pan in place but do not add water. Optionally, line the water pan with aluminum foil for easy cleanup.

Adjust the bottom three intake vents and the single top exhaust vent to 100 percent open. The smoker should come up to the 325 to 350°F (170 to 180°C) range over the next 30 minutes. Once the smoker is above 325°F (170°C), put the pork shoulder on the smoker skin side up. Adjust the bottom vents to maintain the 300 to 325°F (150 to 170°C) temperature. Only if the smoker is running significantly too hot should you adjust the top vent.

Depending on weather conditions and the quality of your charcoal, you may need to add more fuel during this time. Add unlit charcoal via the access door if required.

Cook until a meat thermometer inserted in the thickest part of the shoulder registers 190°F (90°C), about 6 to 8 hours. Test the doneness by checking to see if the meat easily pulls away from the bone. If the bone is still firmly attached to the meat, keep cooking until tender. Move the pork shoulder to a sheet pan with the meat side down and rest for 30 minutes.

Heat a cast iron pan over medium-high heat. Add 1 inch (2.5 cm) of melted lard or vegetable oil to the pan. With a sharp boning knife, carefully remove the skin from the pork shoulder and cut into four pieces. Working in batches, if necessary, crisp the skin in the oil for 3 to 5 minutes per side. Adjust the heat down to medium if the oil starts to smoke. Place the crisped skin onto some newspaper and sprinkle with kosher salt. Proceed to the Pork Skin Sandwich recipe (see page 57) or reserve for serving with the pork shoulder.

Set up a large cutting board and get yourself a large chef's knife. Place the pork shoulder on the cutting board and remove the bone. Process some of the meat into slices. Chop the remaining exterior meat coarsely and the inner white meat finely. If serving the crispy skin with the meat, finely chop the skin and incorporate it with the chopped pork. Season the meat with Western-Style North Carolina Sauce and more kosher salt, to taste. (We start with a ¼ cup [65 g] of the sauce and a tablespoon [14 g] of kosher salt.) No one flavor should be more noticeable than the others. Over generations, North Carolina pitmasters have honed this perfect balance.

Serve the pork to your family and friends right from the cutting board along with some hushpuppies and slaw.

STORAGE
Wrap room temperature leftover pork tightly in plastic wrap. Refrigerate up to 3 days or freeze for up to 1 month.

Pork Skin Sandwich

A pork skin sandwich is certainly not on your cardiologist's list of acceptable foods, but when you find this option hiding on a Western North Carolina menu, it is well worth the temporary spike in your cholesterol numbers. Serve as an appetizer before putting out a pork barbecue spread.

Prep time: 10 minutes
Cook time: No time at all once you've cooked a pork shoulder
Serves: 4

INGREDIENTS
4 soft hamburger buns
Skin from cooked 8 to 10 pound (3.6 to 4.6 kg) picnic shoulder
½ cup (120 ml) Western-Style North Carolina Sauce (see page 74)

IF YOU ARE NOT A PURIST WE ALSO SUGGEST THE FOLLOWING OPTIONAL INGREDIENTS:
Ripe in-season tomato slices
Romaine lettuce leaves
Sliced red onion
Slaw
Sour pickle slices

METHOD
Once the crisped skins are resting on newspaper as detailed in the Western North Carolina Pork Shoulder recipe (see page 55), prepare the sandwiches.

Start by lightly toasting the buns. Add some or all of the optional ingredients if desired. Place a piece of pork skin on each sandwich and drizzle with Western-Style North Carolina Sauce. Top each with the second half of the bun. Cut each sandwich in half and serve immediately.

Hushpuppies Fried in Lard

Traditional North Carolina hushpuppies are a bit on the dense side. Our method isn't traditional. It goes heavy on the baking powder, activated by warm water, to lighten things a little. We suggest going with the plain version when pairing them with barbecue and choosing one of our suggested variations when serving them as an appetizer.

Prep time: 10 minutes
Cook time: 30 minutes
Yield: About 24 hushpuppies

INGREDIENTS

2 cups (275 g) white cornmeal
½ cup (63 g) all purpose flour
2 tablespoons (28 g) baking powder
2 large eggs
½ cup (120 ml) buttermilk

Pinch of kosher salt, plus more to taste
½ cup (120 ml) warm water
3 cups (615 g) lard or (700 ml) vegetable oil

METHOD

In a large mixing bowl, stir together the cornmeal, flour, baking powder, eggs, buttermilk, and a pinch of kosher salt until well blended. Add warm water a little at a time until you have a stiff moist batter. You may not use all the water. Let the batter stand for 10 minutes.

Pour the lard or oil into a heavy-bottomed, straight sided sauté pan or cast iron pot. The oil should be about 3 inches (7.5 cm) deep. Heat the oil to 375°F (190°C).

Drop the batter, a tablespoon (15 g) at a time, into the fry oil. The trick is to use two spoons: one spoon to collect the batter and the other spoon to scrape it out into the fry oil. Work in batches. The hushpuppies won't fry evenly if they are crowded.

Turn the hushpuppies once or twice and fry until golden brown, about 2 minutes. Use a slotted spoon to remove.

Drain on paper or a wire rack. Keep the hushpuppies warm in a 175°F (80°C) oven or serve immediately.

HUSHPUPPY VARIATIONS
Fold in one of the following combinations to a batch of hushpuppy batter before frying. Just don't call these "North Carolina Style."

JALAPEÑO AND CHEESE
¼ cup (40 g) finely chopped sweet white onion
¼ cup (30 g) shredded Cheddar cheese
¼ cup (23 g) minced jalapeño peppers

BACON AND SCALLION
½ cup (40 g) minced cooked bacon
¼ cup (25 g) chopped scallion

SHRIMP AND HATCH CHILE
1 cup (135 g) chopped grilled shrimp
¼ cup (34 g) chopped canned hatch chiles

Homemade Lard

For about as long as people had been eating pigs, lard had been a mainstay cooking oil. But when large corporate food companies introduced new hydrogenated vegetable oil products in the early 1900s, the war on lard began. It fell out of favor in the '50s and '60s as the world of processed foods boomed, but an unassailable truth remained: Potatoes fried in vegetable oil are good, and potatoes fried in lard are glorious.

It's time to welcome lard back into your culinary life. But don't just pick up some shelf lard at the Piggly Wiggly; grab some fatback instead and make your own. The flavor is superior, and you'll produce nice cracklins as a snack.

❋ NOTE: This is a recipe that really benefits from using pasture-fed, heritage-breed pork.

Prep time: 10 minutes
Cook time: 2 hours
Yield: 4 cups lard (820 g) and some cracklins

INGREDIENTS
2 pounds (900 g) unseasoned pork fat, chilled
¼ cup (60 ml) water

METHOD

Dice the chilled fat into 1-inch (2.5 cm) cubes. Place the water and fat into the pot over medium-low heat. Stir every 15 minutes and cook for 2 hours. With a slotted spoon, remove the cracklins. Strain the melted fat through a sieve. Pour the fat into two pint-sized (475 ml) Mason jars. Cool and then cover and refrigerate for up to 1 month.

Return the cracklins to the pot over medium heat and cook until crispy. Salt the cracklins and enjoy a snack.

STORAGE

Refrigerate lard for up to 1 month.

North Carolina Table Sauce

Chop up a pork shoulder and serve this sauce on the side. It allows your hungry crowd to enjoy the pork shoulder *au natural* and then amp up the flavor to their specific tastes. This is not your classic supermarket barbecue sauce. The intent is to provide bright contrast to rich succulent pork barbecue.

Cook time: 20 minutes
Yield: About 3½ cups (825 ml)

INGREDIENTS

2 cups (475 ml) apple cider vinegar
1 cup (320 g) apple or apricot jelly
2 teaspoons coarse black pepper
1 teaspoon crushed red pepper flakes
2 teaspoons kosher salt
1 teaspoon ground cayenne pepper

2 teaspoons Fermented Chile Sauce (see page 62) or Texas Pete Original Hot Sauce
1 teaspoon Worcestershire sauce
½ cup (120 ml) water
1 tablespoon (15 g) light brown sugar

METHOD

Combine all the ingredients in a saucepan over low heat. Bring to a simmer, stirring occasionally. Simmer for 5 minutes. We prefer to serve this warm, drizzled on your chopped pork or served as a side for dipping.

STORAGE

This sauce will last indefinitely in the refrigerator in a tightly sealed container.

Pimento Cheese Spread

Although this recipe actually originated in the North, it is commonly called the "caviar of the South." Pimento cheese spread is most easily described as a magical mixture of cheese, mayo, and pimentos, but each region has its own recipe. It's great on crackers and even better on crackers with Hot Links (see page 133).

Prep time: 10 minutes
Yield: About 3 cups (744 g)

INGREDIENTS

1 cup (225 g) mayonnaise
1½ cups (173 g) shredded sharp yellow
  Cheddar cheese
1 teaspoon garlic powder
¼ teaspoon ground white pepper
1 teaspoon Worcestershire sauce

1 tablespoon (15 ml) Fermented Chile Sauce
  (see page 62) or Frank's RedHot Original
¼ cup (48 g) diced pimento pepper
1 red jalapeño pepper, minced
2 scallion tops, sliced into thin rings
Kosher salt and ground black pepper,
  to taste

METHOD

In a food processor, combine the mayonnaise, Cheddar cheese, garlic powder, white pepper, Worcestershire sauce, and Fermented Chile Sauce. Pulse until fully combined. Transfer the mixture to a bowl and fold in the pimentos, jalapeño, and scallion tops. Season to taste.

STORAGE

Refrigerate in a tightly sealed container for up to 2 weeks.

Homemade Fermented Chile Sauce

When traveling in North Carolina, you run into Texas Pete Original Hot Sauce everywhere. The hot sauce is on every table in every BBQ joint—and for good reason. It's hot, tart flavors are fantastic with smoky pork. Andy wondered if we could recreate this sauce using what he knows about chile fermentation.

The homemade version has an extra brightness and pop. Plus, it's fun to add your own flavors to the sauce. Try making an Asian-style fermented pepper sauce with additions such as garlic, ginger, sugars, fish sauce, or soy sauce.

For chilies, we like anything red. You can choose your own heat level. We use a 50/50 mix of Italian hots and jalapeños, but if habaneros float your boat, then go for it.

Prep time: 45 minutes plus two
   weeks of fermentation
Yield: 3 cups (700 ml)

INGREDIENTS

10 ounces (280 g) fresh red hot chilies,
   green tops removed
¼ cup (60 ml) white vinegar
¼ cup (60 ml) water
1¼ teaspoons kosher salt
¼ teaspoon garlic powder
¼ teaspoon xanthan gum (optional)

METHOD

Place all the ingredients in a blender and purée. Let stand for 30 minutes.

Pour the ingredients in a cylindrical glass jar. The chiles must be fully submerged. If required, use a weight, such as a small glass bowl. Lightly cover the jar with a piece of plastic wrap and poke a few holes in the plastic wrap to let the chiles breathe. Leave the chiles on your counter for two weeks. Stir the chiles after one week. If you see any mold on the surface of the fermentation chiles, simply spoon it out.

After two weeks, transfer the sauce to two pint-sized (475 ml) Mason jars.

Xanthan gum will keep the sauce from separating. Optionally, purée the sauce with the xanthan gum before moving to the Mason jars.

NOTE: If you want to create your own combinations, a solid basic fermenting technique is to add 2 percent salt by weight of the peppers. Press the peppers down and make sure they are covered in liquid and let sit on your counter for at least two weeks.

STORAGE

Refrigerate indefinitely.

"A Definition of Barbecue"

by Sam Jones

SKYLIGHT INN AND SAM JONES BARBECUE

Some people spin a lot of yarn, but I'm not one of those guys. You want to know why we do whole hog? The long and short of it is: whole hog is the way everybody did it.

People in our family have been cooking barbecue for many, many, many generations. My grandfather Pete Jones opened Skylight Inn in Ayden, North Carolina, when he was 17, in the summer of 1947. It was a real joint back then. The parties went on all night. He sold barbecue, hot dogs, hamburgers, whatever he could do to make a buck. But by the late '50s or early '60s, it was all barbecue.

I couldn't change how we do things at Skylight now if I wanted to. Our family is not real big on change—I have two sisters and I'm surprised they don't have the same name. People know what Skylight barbecue tastes like and if I made a switch, they'd know, especially with the chop-style we do. You get the darker part of the meat at the shoulder, the leaner string of the meat at the hams, and the meat of the belly. I'm not saying that's the definition of barbecue, but that's the definition of Eastern North Carolina barbecue to me.

There's never been a time when barbecue was not a part of my life. That restaurant has been the pivot point of our family forever. I hated to work in the restaurant as a kid. The first time I started to see it differently was in college. I had a writing assignment in English class and my thought process was—like most college students— how can I accomplish this with the least amount of effort? I decided to write about barbecue. While I was doing the project, talking to my family, getting dates and people's names, I started looking at things differently. Barbecue's a way of life, not a job.

I started really working at Skylight in 1998. Randomly, one night when I was mopping the floor—this must have been

---

Meat cooked over wood coal is the purest form of food I think I've ever eaten.

---

early 2004—my grandfather stopped me. He wanted to show me how he went about doing things in the restaurant. It was very unlike him to do that, but if he hadn't, I wouldn't be here now. About four months later, on a Sunday, my grandfather had a heart attack. In the hospital that day, he said to me, "Look, I'm probably going to be down for a while. Can you take care of things?"

He never came back to the business. I just had to figure things out. Our customers were always asking about him: "How is your grandfather?

Tell him we're praying for him." But when he passed away in February 2006, public perception changed overnight. Suddenly it was, "The barbecue just isn't same anymore." That was a tough time. We just kept our heads down and hoped it would get better.

We started to get some calls. Someone wanted to make a documentary about us. Southern food expert John T. Edge wanted me to cook at an event at Charleston. I said yeah, but in my mind I was thinking, "There's no way in hell I'm going to go to Charleston and cook pig, 'cause no one in my family had ever cooked away from Ayden, North Carolina. Nobody." But I went down there and when we brought the pig to the front of the restaurant, people stood and applauded. A light bulb went off: "Hey man, there are some people who actually care about what you are doing." That's when we started to redefine who we were, to make a name for ourselves. No longer did we have to ride on my grandfather's coattails.

Some things will never change, though: Meat cooked over wood coal is the purest form of food I think I've ever eaten. It's not a fast process and it's not the easiest, but that's what we do. It's a pure, unbastardized, unadulterated way of cooking that you cannot reproduce any other way. You can't cut a corner and get that same result.

A NORTH CAROLINA STANDARD

SAM JONES
Wood-Fired
N.C.

WHOLE HOG BBQ

Skylight Inn Cornbread

Locally milled cornmeal, water, salt, and lard—as with most things at the Skylight Inn in Ayden, North Carolina, simple is best. There are no jalapeños or buttermilk or Cheddar cheese in this rendition. Instead, this unleavened cornbread is designed to celebrate the flavor of local corn and provide the perfect vehicle to sop up pork barbecue juices. Make the effort to source Southeast cornmeal, there are plenty of mail order options available for those not living near North Carolina.

Prep time: 15 minutes
Cook time: 45 minutes
Serves: 12

INGREDIENTS

2 pounds (900 g) Abbitt's Yellow Corn Meal
   or other fine cornmeal grown and milled
   in the Southeastern United States
2 teaspoons table salt
About 3½ cups (825 ml) water
2 tablespoons (26 g) lard

SPECIAL EQUIPMENT

12-inch (30 cm) cast iron pan

METHOD

Preheat the oven to 350°F (180°C, or gas mark 4). Sift the cornmeal and salt into a large bowl. Slowly mix the water into the cornmeal until the batter is a consistency that would just pour out of a cup. (You might not use all the water.)

Heat the cast iron pan over medium heat for 3 minutes. Turn off the heat and add the lard. Tilt the pan to evenly distribute the lard and then pour in the batter. Bake for 45 minutes. Remove from the oven and let cool. Use a spatula to loosen the cornbread from the pan and flip it onto a cutting board. Slice into 12 wedges and serve.

STORAGE

Wrap in aluminum foil and store in a cool, dark place for up to 3 days. Rewarm in a toaster or the oven for 5 minutes before serving.

How to Cook a Whole Hog Eastern North Carolina Style

Making an Eastern North Carolina whole hog is a simple process in theory: cook a salted pig over a low charcoal fire for 12 to 14 hours and then crank the heat up for the last 30 minutes until the skin is golden and blistered. But it is also an art form that is very difficult to truly master. Cooking a whole hog Eastern North Carolina style is not a set-and-forget process. The magic is in the way you manipulate the coals to ensure slow, even cooking.

We applaud you if you have an open pit and burn barrel setup in your backyard. That was pitmaster Sam Jones's advice to us: "I'd start by buying a mess of cinderblocks and build an open pit." But in this recipe, we strive to provide guidance on how to reliably emulate an Eastern North Carolina–style pig on whatever pit happens to be sitting out in your yard.

Follow these guidelines to bring some predictability to your first few pig cooks. Always target the pig to be done 1 to 2 hours before you'd like to devour it so you don't have a bunch of hungry people milling about and drinking too much beer on an empty stomach. After guests thank you profusely with pig grease gleaming on their chins, feel free to graduate up to the more free-form open pit cooking.

Prep time: 2 hours

COOK TIMES:

At 250°F (120°C): 12 to 14 hours
At 275°F (140°C): 10 to 12 hours
At 300°F (130°C): 8 to 10 hours
At 325°F (170°C): 6 to 8 hours

Serves: 20

INGREDIENTS

1 pig (40 to 60 pounds, or 18.2 to 27.3 kg), split with skin on and hooves removed
½ cup (112 g) kosher salt
About 1 cup (288 g) table salt
About 4 cups (946 ml) Eastern-Style North Carolina Sauce (see page 74)

SPECIAL EQUIPMENT

Two large, full-size sheet pans (optional)

METHOD

Identify the radiant heat characteristic of your pit. Some pits produce more radiant heat on top of the meats and some pits produce radiant heat from below. To test, place two uncooked biscuits on the smoker grate. A top heat pit will produce more color on the top of the biscuit and a bottom heat pit will produce more color on the bottom of the biscuit.

In addition, different pits have different sweet spots for target temperatures. Your temp sweet spot is simply where the smoker likes to settle in when burning a clean fire producing an almost invisible smoke from the stack. You should fire up your pit to that sweet spot range. Overshooting 25 to 50°F (5 to 10 °C) is a good idea as the pit will drop in temp when the whole raw pig is put on.

Place the pig skin side down on an aluminum foil covered table. With your hands, grab the edges of the rib

The magic is in the way you manipulate the coals to ensure slow, even cooking.

cage and press down firmly until the pig lays flat. Some of the rib bones around the sternum should pop. Season the meat side with the kosher salt. Flip the pig skin side up and evenly distribute the table salt on the skin. Crimp aluminum foil around the ears to keep them from burning. Let the pig sit unrefrigerated for 1 hour.

For a top heat pit, position the pig skin side down. For a bottom heat pit, position the pig skin side up. We'll sometimes choose to use a full size sheet pan to help with moving the pig in and out of the cooker. It's really up to you based on the type of smoker you are using. Toss out any aluminum foil that the raw pig was sitting on.

Keep your smoker locked in at the target temperature.

Cook until the hams read 165 to 170°F (75 to 80°C) internal temperature. With insulated gloved hands, carefully flip the pig—you'll likely need at least one helper. Using two full-size sheet pans helps with this task. Slide one underneath the hog and place the other on top. Hold the edges of the pans together tightly and flip.

Return the pig to the pit until 190°F (90°C) is measured in the deepest portion of the ham. Crank up your pit an extra 50 to 100°F (10 to 40°C) and cook for ½ hour to further crisp and blister the skin. Move the pig to the table and let sit for 30 minutes. Chop the skin and meat with two large chefs or butcher knives. Mix the pork and skin and season with Eastern-Style North Carolina Sauce and more kosher salt—taste, taste, taste! It's all about a perfect blend of pig, salt, sauce, and smoke. The simplest ingredients are mind blowing when perfectly balanced.

STORAGE

Wrap room temperature leftover pork tightly in plastic wrap. Refrigerate for up to 3 days or freeze for up to 1 month.

Day Drinking with Sweet Tea

We're heathen types and have been known to partake in the Devil's Juice. If you want to join us, may we suggest doctoring your sweet tea with bourbon and Campari? (For a lower alcohol version, skip the bourbon.) Be forewarned, more than two and you may burn the hog.

Prep time: 10 minutes
Yield: 1

INGREDIENTS
Crushed ice
2 ounces (60 ml) of your favorite bourbon
1 ounce (28 ml) Campari
Couple of dashes of walnut bitters
Sweet tea, to fill the glass

METHOD
Fill a pint (475 ml) glass with crushed ice and add the liquors and bitters. Fill the remaining space with sweet tea, give a quick stir, and enjoy.

SWEET TEA

Many barbecue restaurants in North Carolina are in the Bible Belt: closed on Sundays and instead of bottled beer, patrons drink sweet team from large Styrofoam cups filled with crushed ice. We suggest ditching the Styrofoam for a real glass, but the crushed ice is a must.

Prep time: 15 minutes
Yield: 1 gallon (3.8 L)

INGREDIENTS
4 cups (946 ml) water plus 12 cups (2.8 L) cold water, divided
¼ cup (85 g) honey
¾ cup (150 g) granulated sugar
½ teaspoon whole black peppercorns
2 whole cloves
1 teaspoon grated orange zest
10 bags of black tea
Crushed ice, for serving
Lemon wedges, for serving

METHOD
In a 2-quart (1.9 L) saucepan over high heat, combine 4 cups (946 ml) water, honey, sugar, peppercorns, cloves, and orange zest, stirring occasionally until the mixture boils. Remove from the heat and add the tea bags. Give it a quick swirl and then let it sit for 5 minutes. Strain the liquid through a fine mesh sieve into a 1-gallon (3.8 L) pitcher and add the remaining 12 cups (2.8 L) of cold water. Refrigerate until serving. Serve over crushed ice. A lemon wedge is always nice.

STORAGE
Keep refrigerated for up to 5 days.

North Carolina Sauce

Here lies one of the distinct differences between Eastern North Carolina–style barbecue and Western North Carolina–style barbecue. Both sauces provide a bracing acidity that balances rich, unctuous, fatty pork, but Eastern is spicier and Western adds ketchup for a bit more sweetness.

EASTERN-STYLE NORTH CAROLINA SAUCE

Prep time: 10 minutes
Yield: 3 cups (700 ml)

INGREDIENTS

3 cups (700 ml) apple cider vinegar
1 tablespoon (4 g) crushed red pepper flakes
1 tablespoon (15 ml) Texas Pete Original Hot Sauce
1 tablespoon (15 g) light brown sugar
1 teaspoon table salt
1 teaspoon ground black pepper

METHOD

Place all the ingredients into a quart-sized (946 ml) glass Mason jar. Tightly cover and shake vigorously.

STORAGE

Refrigerate indefinitely.

WESTERN-STYLE NORTH CAROLINA SAUCE

Prep time: 10 minutes
Yield: 1 quart (946 ml)

INGREDIENTS

3 cups (700 ml) apple cider vinegar
¾ cup (180 g) ketchup
1 tablespoon (15 ml) Texas Pete Original Hot Sauce
1 tablespoon (15 g) light brown sugar
1 teaspoon table salt
1 teaspoon ground black pepper

METHOD

Place all the ingredients into a quart-sized (946 ml) glass Mason jar. Tightly cover and shake vigorously.

STORAGE

Refrigerate indefinitely.

Red Slaw

Red slaw or white slaw? It's hard to choose. But in the end, we tend to lean toward the red for the spice, especially paired with the sweetness of smoked pork shoulder on a cheap white roll. There are three elements that are vital to the integrity of a traditional red slaw: the crunch, the zip of the apple cider vinegar, and the funky spiciness of Texas Pete Original Hot Sauce (or our Fermented Chile Sauce).

Prep time: 30 minutes
Serves: 10 to 12 as a side

INGREDIENTS

½ cup (120 g) ketchup
2 tablespoons (26 g) granulated sugar
1 tablespoon (15 g) light brown sugar
1 tablespoon (15 ml) Fermented Chile Sauce
 (see page 62) or Texas Pete Original Hot Sauce
3 dashes of Tabasco Original Red Sauce
½ cup (120 g) apple cider vinegar
1 teaspoon crushed red pepper flakes
1 pinch of ground cayenne pepper
6 cups (540 g) minced green cabbage
1 carrot, peeled and minced
Kosher salt and freshly cracked black
 pepper, to taste

METHOD

In a large mixing bowl, mix together the ketchup, granulated sugar, light brown sugar, Fermented Chile Sauce, Tabasco Sauce, vinegar, crushed red pepper flakes, and cayenne pepper. Add the cabbage and carrot, mix well, and season with kosher salt and pepper to taste.

STORAGE

Refrigerate up to three days in a covered container.

White Slaw

This recipe may be a little controversial. It uses mayo when many North Carolina joints choose to use vinegar only in their preparations. But this version is fantastic directly on a pork sandwich, evenly dispersed in each bite. Think potato chips on a tuna fish sandwich: pure perfection.

Prep time: 45 minutes
Serves: 10 to 12 as a side

INGREDIENTS

½ of a medium green cabbage, cored

1 medium carrot, peeled and minced

1 small yellow onion, peeled and minced

1 cup (225 g) mayonnaise (Duke's Mayonnaise is best, if you can find it.)

1 tablespoon (15 ml) apple cider vinegar

1 tablespoon (13 g) granulated sugar

1 teaspoon onion powder

½ teaspoon Texas Pete Original Hot Sauce

½ teaspoon celery seed

½ teaspoon ground white pepper

Kosher salt, to taste

METHOD

Working in batches, pulse the green cabbage in a food processor until it is evenly minced, pushing down the cabbage from the sides if needed. Transfer the cabbage to a large mixing bowl. Repeat with the remaining cabbage and then mince the carrot and onion the same way, placing them in the same mixing bowl.

In a separate bowl, combine the remaining ingredients and mix well.

Pour the dressing over the minced slaw and mix well. Taste and re-season with kosher salt as necessary. Let sit for 30 minutes or overnight in the refrigerator. Before serving, taste and season with kosher salt or additional vinegar. Serve cold.

STORAGE

Refrigerate in covered container for up to 3 days.

Lexington-Style Cheerwine Pork Shoulder

Our good friend Chris Prieto, pitmaster of PRIME Barbecue in Wendell, North Carolina, is a dedicated student of North Carolina barbecue. And while he has the utmost respect for the classics, he is not afraid to develop new ideas. This recipe is a mashup of regional ingredients —namely Cheerwine (a cherry-flavored soft drink) and Texas Pete Original Hot Sauce—with competition-style techniques. While not classic, we think the results are delicious.

Prep time: 3 to 6 hours
Cook time: 8 to 10 hours
Serves: 12 to 16

INGREDIENTS

1 bone-in whole pork shoulder
  (14 to 18 pounds, or 6.4 to 8.2 kg)
2 cans (12 ounces, or 355 ml each) of
  Cheerwine, divided
¼ cup (60 ml) white vinegar
¼ cup (50 g) granulated sugar
1 tablespoon (15 ml) Texas Pete Original Hot Sauce
½ cup (112 g) kosher salt
1 cup (235 ml) Cheerwine BBQ Sauce, warmed
  (see page 80)

SPECIAL EQUIPMENT

Meat injector
Spray bottle
Wood selection: hickory and cherry blend

METHOD

Trim any excess hard fat from the meaty side of the pork shoulder, but leave the skin side intact. In a bowl, combine 1 can of Cheerwine, vinegar, and sugar. Mix well. With a meat injector, inject the Cheerwine mixture into the pork shoulder at 1-inch (2.5 cm) intervals along the meat side. Wrap in plastic wrap and refrigerate the injected pork shoulder for 2 hours.

Remove the pork shoulder from the refrigerator, dry it off completely with paper towels, and apply a liberal coating of kosher salt to the skin side. Return it to the refrigerator for a minimum of 1 hour and a maximum of 4 hours. Preheat the smoker to between 275 and 300°F (140 to 150°C) using a combination of wood and charcoal. Follow our instructions for charcoal cookers on page 16. Place the pork directly on the center of the grill rack. Close the smoker and adjust the vents and exhaust to maintain a consistent 275°F (140°C).

Pour the remaining can of Cheerwine into the spray bottle. Spray the outside of pork shoulder with the Cheerwine every hour starting on the 1 hour mark. Cook for about 6 hours or until a meat thermometer inserted into thickest portion registers 165 to 170°F (75 to 80°C). Remove the pork from the smoker and double wrap it in heavy-duty aluminum foil. This is a good time to refuel the smoker if needed. Return the wrapped pork shoulder to the smoker and continue cooking until a meat thermometer inserted into thickest portion registers 200°F (95°C), about 2 additional hours. Remove the pork shoulder from the smoker and open the aluminum foil to release excess heat for 5 minutes. Rewrap and let it stand in the aluminum foil for 1 hour at room temperature. Remove the pork from the aluminum foil, reserving any drippings, and place it on a cutting board. In a bowl, mix the Cheerwine BBQ Sauce with the drippings. Pull the meat into large chunks and discard all visible fat and bone. Coarsely chop the meat and drizzle with the Cheerwine BBQ mixture. Serve immediately.

STORAGE

Wrap room temperature leftover pork tightly in plastic wrap. Refrigerate for up to 3 days or freeze up to 1 month.

Cheerwine BBQ Sauce

The combination of Cheerwine and whiskey makes a really outstanding cocktail. And in our experience, anything that mixes well with whiskey also mixes well with barbecue. You can use this sauce with the Lexington-Style Cheerwine Pork Shoulder (see page 79) or as a rib glaze.

Prep time: 10 minutes
Cook time: 30 minutes
Yield: 2 cups (475 ml)

INGREDIENTS

1 can (12 ounces, or 355 ml) of Cheerwine
¾ cup (150 g) granulated sugar
¼ cup (85 g) blackstrap molasses
2 tablespoons (28 ml) red wine vinegar
1 teaspoon kosher salt
1 teaspoon hickory liquid smoke
½ teaspoon crushed red pepper flakes
¼ teaspoon ground cayenne pepper

METHOD

Combine all of the ingredients in a medium saucepan over medium heat. Bring to a simmer and then reduce the temperature to low and simmer for 30 minutes. Let the sauce cool and then transfer to a pint-sized (475 ml) Mason jar.

STORAGE

Refrigerate for up to 3 months

Barbecue Chicken with Skin Cracklins

You won't find this preparation on traditional North Carolina barbecue joint menus. Chris was so inspired by pitmasters who blend crispy skin into chopped pork that he tried the method on chicken. The results are delicious. It's not authentic, but the simplicity of the ingredients—chicken, salt, and vinegar—is very North Carolina.

Prep time: 20 minutes
Cook time: 3 hours
Serves: 6 to 8

INGREDIENTS

4 skin-on, bone-in chicken leg quarters
4 teaspoons (19 g) kosher salt, plus more to taste
1 cup (205 g) lard
½ cup (120 ml) Western-Style North Carolina Sauce (see page 74)

SPECIAL EQUIPMENT

12-inch (30 cm) cast iron pan

METHOD

Season both sides of the chicken leg quarters with kosher salt, about a ½ teaspoon per side. Rest the chicken at room temperature for 30 minutes. While the chicken is resting, prepare your smoker for a 250°F (120°C) 2 hour cook. Once your smoker is a steady 250°F (120°C), cook the chicken skin side down for 2 hours or until meat thermometer inserted near the joint of thigh and leg reads 165°F (75°C). Remove the chicken and let it rest for 15 minutes.

Meanwhile, heat the lard in a cast iron pan over medium heat. The lard should be about a ½-inch (1.3 cm) deep. Remove the skin from the chicken. Fry one piece of skin at a time until crispy, about 2 to 3 minutes per side. Rest the crisped skins on crumpled newspaper and sprinkle with a bit of kosher salt. Using your hands or two forks, pull the meat off of the chicken bones and break it into thumb-sized pieces. Chop the chicken skins on a cutting board. Mix the chicken and crisped skins together while dressing with the Western-Style North Carolina Sauce. Taste and adjust the seasoning with additional kosher salt or sauce.

Serve immediately in small paper boats.

STORAGE

Wrap room temperature leftover chicken tightly in plastic wrap. Refrigerate up to 3 days or freeze up to 1 month.

Brunswick Stew

All sorts of critters—rabbits, chickens, squirrels—could be used to fix up a fine pot of Brunswick stew. Leftover pork barbecue may be more readily on hand though and it's what we call for in this recipe. Warm up a pot of this stew when you need to stay warm on a cold night tending the pit. While many barbecue joints use frozen vegetables, we greatly prefer fresh.

Prep time: 15 minutes
Cook time: 45 minutes
Serves: 8 to 10

INGREDIENTS

2 tablespoons (28 ml) vegetable oil
1 large sweet onion, diced
1 large carrot, diced
2 cloves of garlic, minced
3 cups (700 ml) pork or chicken stock
1 can (14.5 ounces, or 410 g) of diced tomatoes
1 cup (250 g) IQUE Sauce v2.0 (see page 197) or your favorite barbecue sauce
½ cup (120 g) ketchup
2 tablespoons (28 ml) Worcestershire sauce
1 tablespoon (20 g) blackstrap molasses
1 tablespoon (15 ml) apple cider vinegar
1 teaspoon crushed red pepper flakes
1 teaspoon kosher salt
½ teaspoon dried thyme
1 bay leaf
2 pounds (900 g) chopped pork barbecue
2 cups (312 g) fresh lima beans (or substitute [328 g] frozen lima beans)
3 ears of corn, husked and kernels removed
Kosher salt and black pepper, to taste
Skylight Inn Cornbread (see page 68), or Cornbread with Butter, Honey, and Sea Salt (see page 37), for serving

METHOD

Heat the oil in a large saucepan over medium-high heat for 2 to 3 minutes. Sauté the onion, carrots, and garlic, stirring frequently, until golden brown and softened, about 3 to 4 minutes. Add the stock, canned tomatoes, barbecue sauce, ketchup, Worcestershire sauce, molasses, vinegar, crushed red pepper flakes, kosher salt, dried thyme, and bay leaf. Mix well. Bring to a boil, stirring occasionally, and then reduce heat to medium and simmer uncovered for 5 minutes.

Add the pork, lima beans, and corn kernels. Let simmer uncovered for an additional 20 minutes, stirring occasionally. Season with kosher salt and freshly cracked black pepper to taste. Remove the bay leaf. Serve immediately with warm cornbread.

STORAGE

Refrigerate, covered, for up to 3 days.

"New Barbecue"

Elizabeth Karmel

CAROLINA CUE TO-GO

I fell in love with barbecue because it's not only a way to cook, it's a community. And as far as I'm concerned, there's room for everybody and every style. To me, barbecue has always been about how delicious it is.

The only rule of barbecue is wood . . . It's not true barbecue unless it has a kiss of wood smoke.

I grew up in North Carolina and I was known for my North Carolina–style barbecue. Then, I opened Hill Country Barbecue Market in New York, serving Teas-style barbecue. Now, I have an online barbecue shack called CarolinaCue To-Go, a mash-up of Eastern North Carolina–style whole hog and my Western North Carolina–style sauce. I think tradition is essential—but I also think this is the best North Carolina barbecue I've ever had.

Understanding the origins of barbecue is really important. But it's equally important for us to recognize the evolution of barbecue. I feel very strongly about food traditions. They make up who we are as people. As a Southerner who left the South, a lot of my identity has to do with the food I grew up with. But what I'm doing at Carolina Cue To-Go is not traditional. I don't want anyone to think that it is. We need to do a better job differentiating between the traditional legendary barbecue and this new way of cooking. We need history and perspective, but we can also celebrate new ideas and new ways of doing things. We should give them a moniker like "New Barbecue," the way that the French coined *haute cuisine*.

Look at central Texas. There is a whole new generation of pitmasters that is changing things. They are wrapping their meat, so it steams. It's much more succulent than the traditional open-pit, drier Central Texas barbecue.

And if you only read the headlines and don't get into the nitty gritty, you would think that some of these young upstarts are the best barbecue in Texas. What we should be saying is that they are the best of a new generation of pitmasters in Texas. Texas has barbecue restaurants that are 150 years old, pitmasters who have been in business for three or four generations and they've been cooking in the same pit and using the same techniques for that long. We need to be proud of that and talk about that, too.

To me, the only rule of barbecue is wood. It's a necessary flavoring ingredient. You absolutely have to use wood. That is the distinction between grilling and barbecue; the food has to have a touch of smoke.

I have no problem with an electric fan-assisted grill. Some people say it's not a real smoker if you have to use electricity, but I think it's okay. And I don't think there's any problem with a gas assist. We're just too quick to say "that's not a real barbecue restaurant" because it uses a gas-assist smoker. But it's not true barbecue unless it has a kiss of wood smoke.

Butterflied Grilled Duck with Spicy Watermelon Glaze

Not everything in North Carolina is pork and vinegar. Elizabeth Karmel is one of the best grillers we know and here is her fabulous duck and watermelon recipe. The key is setting up your grill for indirect yet medium high heat—around 325°F (170°C). A kamado–style ceramic smoker, such as a Big Green Egg, is the perfect grill for this recipe.

Prep time: 20 minutes
Cook time: 2½ hours
Serves: 4 to 6

INGREDIENTS

2 whole ducks (4 to 5 pounds, or
   1.8 to 2.3 kg each)
Olive oil, as needed
½ teaspoon kosher salt
Freshly ground black pepper, as needed
2 cups (475 ml) Spicy Watermelon Glaze
   (see page 89)

METHOD

Remove the ducks from the packaging and pat dry with paper towels. Using poultry or kitchen shears, cut along each side of the back bone and remove it. Turn the duck breast side up. Open the two sides of the duck as if you were opening a book and lay it flat. Break the breast bone by firmly applying pressure and pressing down—you may break a few rib bones in the process. Tuck the wing tip under the upper wing and place on a sheet pan.

Prepare your smoker or grill for indirect cooking. Target 300 to 325°F (150 to 170°C) and add a few chunks of hardwood to your charcoal bed when the ducks go on.

Brush the ducks all over with olive oil. Season lightly on both sides with kosher salt and black pepper. Place the ducks skin side up in the center of the grill or a smoker and let cook for about 2 hours before glazing.

After two hours, brush the glaze on the ducks. Continue cooking for 20 to 30 more minutes, brushing with the glaze 2 more times during the final grilling time. Cook until the juices run clear and the thigh registers 190°F (90°C).

Remove the ducks from the grill; brush with glaze one last time and let rest for 10 minutes. Cut the duck into halves or quarters and serve.

STORAGE
Wrap room temperature leftover duck tightly in plastic wrap. Refrigerate for up to 3 days or freeze for up to 1 month.

SPICY WATERMELON GLAZE

Prep time: 15 minutes
Cook time: 15 minutes
Yield: 1 quart (946 ml)

INGREDIENTS
4 cups (600 g) watermelon chunks (about ½ of a small watermelon)
1 jar (12 ounces, or 340 g) apple jelly
Juice and zest of 1 small lime
2 teaspoons crushed red pepper flakes
1 teaspoon jalapeño hot sauce
Pinch of kosher salt

METHOD
Place the watermelon on a food mill or juicer and collect the juice. You should have about 1 cup (235 ml) of juice. Discard the seeds and solid bits.

Put the apple jelly in a small, heavy-bottomed saucepan over low heat. Melt the jelly, stirring occasionally so that it doesn't burn. When the jelly is melted, add the watermelon juice and stir to combine. Add the lime juice and zest and stir again. Add the crushed red pepper flakes, jalapeño hot sauce, and kosher salt. Mix and taste, adjusting the seasoning if desired.

You can use warm or let cool and transfer to a clean jar.

STORAGE
The glaze will keep tightly covered in the refrigerator for up to 2 days.

Kansas City

" . . . So that truth, justice, excellence in Barbecue and the American way of life may be strengthened and preserved forever."

—KANSAS CITY BARBECUE SOCIETY JUDGES OATH

The United States is a diverse country, and there are many different opinions on the definition of the "American way of life" enshrined in the Kansas City Barbecue Society oath. But no matter your point of view, it's hard to argue that democracy is not one of the most important aspects.

No region represents barbecue democracy better than Kansas City. The Kansas City barbecue scene is chock full of old-time joints, new-school restaurants, backyarders, competition teams for miles, and everything in between. The ultimate barbecue convention is the American Royal Open held in Kansas City each October. The event is a come-one, come-all barbecue mecca where over 600 teams compete, celebrate, and break bread. Quite possibly the most patriotic moment of our lives was when we stood in the America Royal arena with thousands of barbecue compadres listening to a twelve-year-old girl from the local 4H chapter sing the national anthem.

Kansas City is a melting pot of not only barbecue people but also barbecue styles. Texas beef barbecue and Memphis-style pork barbecue meld together in delicious ways, creating something that is both traditional and unique. Quite possibly the most populist and delicious dish in the world of American barbecue is Kansas City burnt ends. Traditionally crafted from humble cutting-board scraps, it has been elevated to a dish of great regional pride and a standard bearer by which all Kansas City restaurants are judged.

So don't hesitate. The barbecue world is open to everyone. Just let the gas grill sit idle for the summer, burn a clean fire, and do your part to keep an American culinary treasure alive and well.

Kansas City Tribute Sauce

This sauce is probably the most maligned barbecue sauce out there. So many barbecue joints in Kansas City have developed wonderfully balanced, perfect examples of classic American barbecue sauce, but the commercial stuff found on supermarket shelves across the country is unfortunately too sweet and gloopy, and it's riddled with liquid smoke. Here is our tribute to a great American classic.

Prep time: 30 minutes
Cook time: 30 minutes
Yield: 2 quarts (1.9 L)

INGREDIENTS FOR SPICE MIX:

¼ cup (30 g) chili powder
1 tablespoon (7 g) paprika
2 teaspoons garlic powder
2 teaspoons kosher salt
2 teaspoons ground black pepper
1 teaspoon dried thyme
1 teaspoon chipotle powder
1 teaspoon mustard seed
¼ teaspoon celery seed
Pinch of ground cloves

FOR SAUCE:

2 tablespoons (28 ml) vegetable oil
1 medium yellow onion, minced
4 cloves of garlic, minced
1 cup (235 ml) white vinegar
½ cup (170 g) blackstrap molasses
½ cup (115 g) brown sugar
1 tablespoon (11 g) yellow mustard
4 cups (720 g) crushed canned tomatoes
2 cups (475 ml) water
1 cup (240 g) ketchup
¼ cup (65 g) tomato paste
2 tablespoons (28 ml) Worcestershire sauce

METHOD

Whisk the spice mix ingredients together in a mixing bowl. Optionally, pulse the mixture in a spice grinder for 30 seconds to ensure maximum blending. Transfer to an airtight container.

Combine the oil, onion, and garlic in a medium saucepan over medium-low heat. Cook, stirring occasionally, until the onions and garlic are golden brown, about 5 to 7 minutes. Add the spice mixture and give it a good stir. Add the vinegar, molasses, brown sugar, and mustard and stir again. Increase the heat to medium high and bring the mixture to a boil, stirring frequently to make sure nothing is stuck to the bottom of the pan. Once the mixture boils, lower the heat to medium and simmer for 2 more minutes. Add the crushed tomatoes, water, ketchup, tomato paste, and Worcestershire sauce and continue to simmer, stirring occasionally, for 10 minutes.

Cool the sauce to room temperature and purée in a blender.

STORAGE

Refrigerate for up to 1 month.

Burnt Ends

Burnt ends are traditionally made from the brisket point, which can be difficult to source. Typically, you can only find it still attached to a brisket flat. A good butcher may be able to fabricate this cut for you (in butcher speak, the cut is known as "NAMP/IMPS 120B") or you can buy a whole packer brisket and remove the point yourself. Save the flat for Beef Barbecue (see page 29) or Montreal Smoked Meat (see page 149). You can also cook a whole brisket and remove the point once it reaches 200°F (95°C) internal temperature and then skip forward to the part of the recipe that calls for the meat to be cubed. Another option—though it's not classic Kansas City—is to use beef chuck, which is widely available and produces excellent burnt ends.

If using a Weber Smoky Mountain Cooker or other water smoker, consider running the water pan empty. (Be sure to line the pan with a few layers of aluminum foil.) This recipe really benefits from a dry cooking environment. The goal is crunchy, crispy bark.

Prep time: 10 minutes
Cook time: 6 to 8 hours
Serves: 4 to 6

INGREDIENTS

1 brisket point or chuck roast (4 to 6 pounds, or 1.8 to 2.7 kg), trimmed of all exterior fat
½ cup (50 g) plus 2 tablespoons (16 g) Classic Kansas City Dry Rub
½ cup (125 g) Kansas City Tribute Sauce

METHOD

Prepare your smoker for a 275°F (140°C) 8 hour cook.

Remove the meat from the refrigerator. Apply ½ cup (50 g) of the Classic Kansas City Dry Rub to all sides of the beef. Once the smoker is ready, add the beef to the smoker. Close the lid and cook without peeking for 2 hours. After 2 hours, flip the beef and cook for another 1 hour. Check the internal temperature. Keep cooking the beef until the internal temperature is 200°F (95°C). You'll be close to this goal after 4 hours with a smaller chuck roast and 6 hours for a larger brisket point. When the internal temperature reaches 200°F (95°C), remove the meat from the smoker and place it on a cutting board to cool slightly.

In a saucepan over low heat, warm the Kansas City Tribute Sauce.

After the beef has cooled enough to handle, slice the meat into 1-inch (2.5 cm) cubes. Add the cubes to an aluminum pan. Drizzle the sauce on top and sprinkle in the remaining 2 tablespoons (16 g) of Classic Kansas City Dry Rub. Toss to combine. Return the pan to the smoker and cook for 1 hour.

Serve with sliced white bread and Pickled Onions (see page 127).

STORAGE

Wrap leftover burnt ends tightly in plastic wrap. Refrigerate for up to 3 days or freeze for up to 1 month.

Butterfly Pork Butt Burnt Ends

Yes, Kansas City burnt ends are always made with the point of the beef brisket. However, the pork butt possesses many of the same characteristics of a beef brisket point. Both the butt and the point are heavily marbled and almost impossible to overcook. Pork butts are also quite a bit cheaper and easier to procure. Trust us; give this one a try.

Prep time: 30 minutes
Cook time: 8 hours
Serves: 12

INGREDIENTS

1 boneless Boston butt pork shoulder
  (6 to 8 pounds, or 2.7 to 3.6 kg)
¾ cup (75 g) Classic Kansas City Dry Rub
  (see page 98), divided
¼ cup (48 g) turbinado sugar
1 cup (250 g) Kansas City Tribute Sauce
  (see page 93)

METHOD

Place the pork butt fat side down on the cutting board. Position a large sharp slicing knife parallel to the cutting board. Slice the pork butt partially in half starting from the end where the shank bone was removed. Stop slicing just short of the "money muscle," the tubular muscle that runs across the butt opposite of the shank bone. Open along the cut. You should now have one long 2- to 3-inch (5 to 7.5 cm) thick piece of pork shoulder. Trim any portions that are significantly thicker. Trim all excess fat from the exterior of the meat.

Sprinkle all sides of the meat with ½ cup (50 g) of the Classic Kansas City Dry Rub and then the ¼ cup (48 g) of sugar. Let the pork sit at room temperature for up to 1 hour as you prepare your smoker for 275 to 300°F (140 to 150°C). Smoke the pork for 6 hours or until it reaches an internal temperature of 180°F (85°C). Remove the pork from the smoker and let it rest

for 20 minutes. Once the pork is cool enough to handle, slice it into even 1- to 2-inch (2.5 to 5 cm) cubes. Place the cubed pork into an aluminum foil pan. Toss with the Kansas City Tribute Sauce and then sprinkle with the remaining ¼ cup (25 g) of Classic Kansas City Dry Rub. Place back on the smoker for an additional 1 to 2 hours until the pork is well caramelized and succulent and meltingly tender. You'll need to eat a piece of the pork burnt ends to check for the proper doneness.

Serve immediately with some cheap white bread, a side of fries, and some pickles.

STORAGE

Wrap room temperature leftover pork tightly in plastic wrap. Refrigerate up to 3 days or freeze up to 1 month.

Classic Kansas City Dry Rub

To us, Kansas City–style dry rub is the quintessential spice mix of classic American barbecue. Many commercially available competition-style rubs are based on a recipe similar to this one. You can add additional ½ teaspoons of intense exotic ingredients like curry powder or espresso powder to suit your own tastes.

Prep time: 15 minutes
Yield: 2 cups (200 g)

INGREDIENTS

½ cup (96 g) turbinado sugar
¼ cup (56 g) kosher salt
¼ cup (28 g) sweet paprika
2 tablespoons (15 g) chili powder
1 tablespoon (6 g) freshly ground black pepper
2 teaspoons onion powder

2 teaspoons garlic powder
1 teaspoon ground cumin
1 teaspoon dry mustard
1 teaspoon celery salt
1 teaspoon MSG (optional)
½ teaspoon lemon pepper
½ teaspoon cayenne pepper

METHOD

Whisk all the ingredients together in a mixing bowl. Optionally, pulse the mixture in a spice grinder for 30 seconds to ensure maximum blending. Transfer to an airtight container.

STORAGE

Store in an airtight container out of the sunlight.

Smoked Prime Rib

Here we employ a double technique. A direct grill creates a wonderful crust, and then the smoker lays on a nice aggressive smoke. You can spin this dish for a celebration dinner or for something more casual like beef sandwiches for a tailgate. Don't skip the Hot Garlic Crunch Cream (see page 101) on the side.

Prep time: 20 minutes
Cook time: 3 to 3½ hours
Serves: 6 to 8 as an entrée

INGREDIENTS

6 cloves of garlic, peeled and smashed
2 tablespoons (28 g) kosher salt
1 tablespoon (6 g) freshly cracked black pepper
2 sprigs of fresh rosemary, leaves chopped
1 teaspoon crushed red pepper flakes
½ cup (120 ml) olive oil
1 bone-in beef prime rib roast (6 pounds, or 2.7 kg)
Hot Garlic Crunch Cream (see page 101)
Side of Fries (see page 112)

SPECIAL EQUIPMENT

Probe thermometer

METHOD

Preheat a gas or charcoal grill to medium-high.

Preheat the smoker to 250°F (120°C) with an aggressive flavored wood such as hickory or pecan.

Place the garlic, kosher salt, black pepper, chopped rosemary leaves, and red pepper flakes into your food processor and blend until smooth. Add the oil and blend to a smooth purée. Place the prime rib on a sheet pan and smear the seasoning paste over the entire roast. Allow to stand for 10 minutes.

Before starting to grill your beef, add the smoke wood to your smoker so it will be kicking out some good smoke when the grilling is done.

Place the rib eye directly over the preheated grill and sear for 3 to 4 minutes until golden brown and caramelized on all sides. Once all sides have been seared, place the prime rib bone side down in your smoker. Insert your remote thermometer probe from the side into the center of the beef eye. Smoke for 2½ to 3 hours until the internal temperature is 130°F (55°C)—this temperature will yield a just-past-medium-rare roast.

Remove the prime rib from the smoker and place on a wire rack fitted over a sheet pan. Let it rest for 15 minutes.

Carve the roast off the bone and then slice the meat into ½-inch (1.3 cm) slabs. Place the sliced meat on a platter, separate the bones with a knife, and place them on the side of the platter. Alternatively, slice thinly and serve with rolls for sandwiches.

Serve hot with Hot Garlic Crunch Cream and a Side of Fries.

STORAGE

Refrigerate for up to 3 days.

Hot Garlic Crunch Cream

This spread adds a complexity to your perfectly smoked prime rib—or to any dish. Crunchy, spicy, and creamy, it won't let you down. Think of it as Lipton onion dip with a Ph.D.

Prep time: 10 minutes
Cook time: 15 minutes
Yield: 2 cups (460 g)

INGREDIENTS

½ cup (120 ml) extra virgin olive oil

10 cloves of garlic, minced

1 tablespoon (4 g) crushed red pepper flakes

1 teaspoon kosher salt

1 cup (230 g) cream cheese, softened

½ cup (115 g) sour cream

1 teaspoon Worcestershire sauce

Additional kosher salt and freshly cracked black pepper, to taste

METHOD

Combine the olive oil, garlic, red pepper flakes, and kosher salt in a saucepan over medium heat. Cook, stirring constantly, with a wooden spoon until the garlic is dark golden brown—the color of cinnamon. You want to make sure the garlic does not stick to the bottom of the pan, so scrape often while stirring. Once the garlic is done, immediately scrape the contents of the pan into a bowl to cool.

Place the cream cheese and sour cream in a stand mixer with a paddle. Mix on low until completely combined and then gradually add in the browned garlic mixture and Worcestershire sauce, mixing well. Taste for seasoning. Add kosher salt and pepper as required.

STORAGE

Refrigerate for up to 1 week.

3-2-1 St. Louis Ribs

This classic barbecue technique has three steps: smoke the meat, wrap it in aluminum foil, and then finish the meat out of the aluminum foil. The most common method calls for low and slow cooking: 3 hours in the smoke, 2 hours in aluminum foil, and 1 hour with the finishing glaze.

But aluminum foil wrapping has a poor reputation with many who bemoan its negative impact on the bark that forms on the outside of the meat. Wrapping the meat softens the bark. The culprit is steam and any liquid the pitmaster adds at this point in the process.

Chris combats this problem two ways. First, he doesn't add any liquid during the two-hour wrap step. And second, he wraps the ribs very tightly, not giving any room for steam to kick up inside of the aluminum foil. These techniques minimize the downside of the method while consistently producing succulent, super tender, crowd-pleasing Kansas City–style ribs.

Prep time: 30 minutes
Cook time: 6 hours
Serves: 6 to 8

INGREDIENTS

2 racks of pork spare ribs, trimmed St. Louis style with the membranes removed (see page 105)
1 cup (100 g) Classic Kansas City Dry Rub (see page 93)
2 cups (500 g) Kansas City Tribute Sauce (see page 93)

SPECIAL EQUIPMENT

Probe thermometer

METHOD

Prepare your smoker for a low and slow cook, 225°F to 235°F (110 to 115°C). For this method, we prefer the Weber Smokey Mountain Cooker, the Big Green Egg, or Humphrey's BBQ Cabinet Smoker, which do a better job at low and slow temperatures compared to offset pits (see page 135).

Place the ribs meat side down on top of a piece of aluminum foil. Sprinkle with ⅓ cup (33 g) of the Classic Kansas City Dry Rub. Flip the ribs and apply another ⅓ cup (33 g) of Classic Kansas City Dry Rub to the meat side. Let the ribs sit at room temperature for 30 minutes until they "sweat" some moisture.

This step is essentially a quick cure that improves the crust on the ribs during the cooking process. Place the ribs on the smoker meat side up and sprinkle with an additional light dusting— about 1 tablespoon (8 g)— of the Classic Kansas City Dry Rub.

Smoke the ribs for 3 hours—no peeking, no misting, no basting! Just maintain a 225 to 235°F (110 to 115°C) cooking temperature for 3 hours.

Wrap the ribs tightly in heavy duty aluminum foil. Seal the rib package tightly to remove any air pockets. Make sure the seal is on the bone side of the ribs.

This is a good time to refuel or refill a water pan if necessary. Return the ribs to the smoker meat side down. Smoke for an additional 2 hours.

After 2 hours, warm the Kansas City Tribute Sauce on your stove. Keep the ribs on the smoker, crack open the aluminum foil, and baste the backside of the ribs. Fold and crimp the edges of the aluminum foil so the ribs are fully exposed but still sitting on the aluminum foil. Close the smoker. After 20 minutes, flip the ribs and baste the meat side. Close the smoker and smoke for an additional 20 minutes. Grind ¼ cup (25 g) of the Classic Kansas City Dry Rub to a fine powder

in a spice grinder. Dust the ribs on the meat side
with the ground rub, close the smoker, and cook for
the final 20 minutes.

Remove the ribs by picking up the edges of the aluminum
foil. Flip the racks onto a cutting board meat side down.
Slice between the bones, stack ribs on a platter, and serve
immediately.

STORAGE
Wrap the room temperature ribs tightly in plastic wrap.
Refrigerate for up to 3 days or freeze for up to 30 days.

Trimming St. Louis Ribs

St Louis trimmed ribs can now be
commonly found in most supermarkets
and butchers shops. When we started
cooking barbecue about 20 years ago,
typically only two options were available
to us—full untrimmed racks of spareribs
or baby back ribs. We learned trimming
down the full spareribs to a uniform
rectangular St. Louis cut is a pretty
simple process and introduces a few key
benefits. Just like with a rack of baby
backs, the uniform shape of St. Louis
ribs cook more evenly, make them easier
to eat, and maximizes the amount of
space available on your smoker. Spareribs are heavily marbled with fat and
tastier than baby backs, in our opinion,
so the St. Louis cut gives the cook the
best of both worlds. Be sure to save the
flap meat from the trimming process—
once a bunch has been accumulated in
your freezer, whip up a batch of hot
links (pg 133).

1.

Place ribs meat-side down and cut away sternum bone.

2.

Cut away flap meat and excess cartilage along of the base of the rib bones.

3.

Cut in straight even lines.

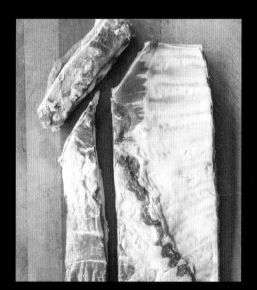

4.

Grab the skin on the back of the bones with a paper towel.

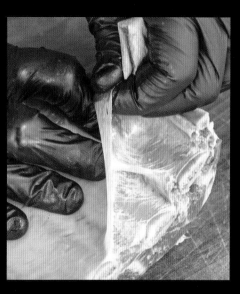

5.

Peel the skin off of the bones.

"Immersed in Barbecue"

by Rod Gray

PELLET ENVY AND EATBARBECUE.COM

In Kansas City, you don't have to earn your way into the barbecue culture. If you put out good food, you quickly rise to the top. We're immersed in barbecue here. We're surrounded by it. The Kansas City style is a little bit of Texas barbecue and a little bit of Memphis and not quite so much of Carolina barbecue. We combined them all to make it our own. As my friend and author Doug Worgul says, "We didn't invent barbecue in Kansas City, we just perfected it."

Before it was barbecue for me, it was golf. I was really into golf, but I finally succumbed to the idea that I was never going to be a great golfer. Still, I needed a hobby. I owned my own business— I was an insurance restoration contractor —and I needed a distraction.

I remember it was 2001 when my office manager and her father invited me to a big barbecue competition. I had no expectations except that I knew it was going to be hot. It was July in Kansas. I expected to see 200 barbecue teams, all absolutely miserable in that heat, but instead I found all these teams having an absolute blast. It was a party. I was just enamored. My wife was out of town that weekend, and I went home and got on the Internet and read about barbecue all night. The sun came up and I was still reading. Two days later, I bought a cooker one state away and stopped to buy two briskets on the way back home— I didn't even know what brisket was then—and that's how I got started.

Barbecue was an awesome distraction from a tough job. I spent more and more time doing it. It got to the point where every Friday, I would sneak off for a contest. And then it was every Thursday because we were traveling a lot. I remember that first year in competition. People were just starting to notice us. I was at a competition in

Kansas City and a couple of guys walked up to me and dove into conversation. They admitted to me that they finished their chicken in a microwave in their trailer and they wanted me to admit the same. They wanted me to admit that we cheated. I didn't know they were teasing me! That's how it goes. We were new.

I want a little sweet, a little heat, a little salt, and a little savory. I want it all, but not too much of any of it.

We hadn't been on the circuit long and we really hadn't been asking anyone for help. We started to win, so people began to take notice.

It took years for me to decide maybe I should do this for a living—even though I was already doing it for a living. I shut down my business on December 31, 2006, after 20 years. The economy had turned on us. I was a little depressed because I hated not being a success, and I kind of wandered around for a couple of months. It wasn't until I was driving home, 12 hours, from Hammond,

Louisiana, having helped Tuffy Stone vend for the first time, that I wrapped my head around the idea of making barbecue my job. The Pellet Envy team was already successful; I decided I would start by offering a barbecue class. A few months later, I got my first sponsor. It really just fell into place.

My whole philosophy about competition barbecue—from day one—has been to offend no one. I think I have an immature palate. If something is bitter or hot or salty, I feel like I experience those things more strongly than the average person. My goal, then, is to create a balanced product. I want a little sweet, a little heat, a little salt, and a little savory. I want it all, but not too much of any of it. And once I found that balance, I haven't been quick to change. Good food is good food, in 2001 or 2016. Now, I've started a rub and barbecue sauce company. I never wanted to be in the barbecue products business. It's hard and there's not much money in it. There were already so many great products on the market. But after I won BBQ Pitmasters, I decided to create the sauces that I use in competition. It's one of the hardest things I've ever done, but it's been rewarding. We started in 53 stores in Kansas City and now we're on shelves around the country. And, of course, I use them every weekend in competition.

Barbecue and bourbon just go hand-in-hand. Joy Richard taught us why they are such a good pair. Her cocktails highlight the ways in which the strong caramel, maple, and toasted flavors of bourbon and rye complement rich, succulent smoked meats.

We first met Joy years ago when she founded the Boston Chapter of Ladies United for the Preservation of Endangered Cocktails (LUPEC), a classic cocktail society dedicated to the "raising, breeding, and releasing of nearly extinct cocktails into the wild."

Joy spent more than a dozen years behind the bar in some of Boston's best whiskey joints and recently relocated to Charleston, South Carolina, where she's creating cocktails for Bar Mash, which has the largest collection of American whiskeys in that city.

Joy tells a great story about the intertwined histories of American whiskey and smoked meat: Some people say that the word "barbecue" comes from an advertisement for an establishment that served smoked meat, liquor, and beer and had pool tables. That's a bar, with beer and cues—bar-be-cue. It might be true, she says, or maybe not, but there is historical precedent for serving American whiskey with barbecue. Both originally came from Southern farms, where corn and rye were grown to feed both the livestock and the stills. So, another barbecue tradition lives on in Joy's recipes in this chapter.

BOURBON COCKTAILS
Bourbon served neat is always a fine choice. Yet, when the barbecue meats are tucked in and the fire is stoked, we like to kick back and relax with a cocktail. The ritual of taking the time to properly stir and serve a cocktail to friends immediately puts us in the perfect barbecue headspace. For cocktails, our favorite bourbons include 10-year Eagle Rare, Bulleit Straight Bourbon, W.L. Weller Special Reserve, and Buffalo Trace.

REMEDY

Serves: 1

INGREDIENTS

1½ ounces (42 ml) rye whiskey
¾ ounce (21 ml) sweet vermouth
   (Cocchi Vermouth di Torino or
   Carpano Antica preferred)
½ ounce (15 ml) Green Chartreuse
¼ ounce (7 ml) Fernet Branca
1 dash of Fee's Black Walnut Bitters

METHOD

Combine all the ingredients in a mixing glass. Add ice and stir for 20 seconds. Strain into a chilled rocks glass and garnish with a grapefruit peel.

WACO OLD FASHIONED

Serves: 1

INGREDIENTS

2 ounces (60 ml) bourbon
½ ounce (15 ml) Dr. Pepper Syrup
3 dashes of orange bitters (Fee's preferred)
1 dash of Fee's Black Walnut Bitters

METHOD

Combine all the ingredients in a mixing glass. Add ice and stir for 20 seconds. Strain over fresh ice into a rocks glass and garnish with an orange peel.

DR. PEPPER SYRUP

Yield: 1 cup (235 ml)

INGREDIENTS

¾ cup (150 g) sugar
¾ cup (175 ml) water
2 cups (475 ml) Dr. Pepper

METHOD

In a sauce pan, bring the water and sugar to a boil. Whisk to dissolve the sugar and then add the Dr. Pepper. Reduce the heat and simmer until reduced by half, stirring occasionally. Let cool completely and store in the refrigerator in an airtight container.

BOURBON BELLE

Serves: 1

INGREDIENTS

2 ounces (60 ml) bourbon
½ ounce (15 ml) sweet vermouth
   (Cinzano Rosso preferred)
½ ounce (15 ml) peach liqueur
   (Mathilde or Giffard preferred)
3 dashes of Angostura bitters

METHOD

Combine all the ingredients in a mixing glass. Add ice and stir for 20 seconds. Strain into a chilled cocktail glass and garnish with a lemon peel.

Pork Rib Sandwich

The Golden Arches version of the pork rib sandwich is beloved by many, yet it is sacrilegious to anyone remotely involved with real barbecue. Here is how to make your own slow-food version that is leaps and bounds better than the fast food rendition. Throw a couple extra racks on during your next rib cook for this recipe.

Prep time: 30 minutes
Cook time: 4 hours
Serves: 4

INGREDIENTS

2 racks of fully cooked St. Louis cut barbecue ribs (see page 105)
4 sub rolls
Kansas City Tribute Sauce (see page 93) or Blues Hog Smokey Mountain Sauce (amount to taste)
½ of a sweet onion, thinly sliced

1 cup (119 g) bread and butter pickles
Side of Fries, for serving (see page 112)

METHOD

At the end of your rib cook process, allocate two racks of ribs for the sandwiches. It's important to conduct the trimming process while the ribs are still hot. Trim away any excess meat and cartilage along the base of the ribs. Remove each rib bone. Some will pop right out easily. Some will require slicing away some of the meat on the back side of the ribs.

Cut the now-boneless ribs into slabs that are slightly bigger than the sub roll. Lightly grill or toast the sub rolls. Place a rib portion on each roll and smear the top of the roll with barbecue sauce. Layer the sliced onion and pickles on the sandwich. Serve with a Side of Fries.

STORAGE

Wrap room temperature leftover sandwiches tightly in plastic wrap. Refrigerate for up to 3 days.

Side of Fries

Making the perfect French fry—crunchy outside, fluffy within—requires double duty with the oil.

Prep time: 30 minutes
Cook time: 30 minutes
Serves: 4 to 6

INGREDIENTS

4 large Russet potatoes
Canola or peanut oil, for frying
Kosher salt or barbecue rub for seasoning

SPECIAL EQUIPMENT

Tall saucepan
Candy thermometer or Thermapen
Wire mesh skimmer or slotted spoon
Wire rack placed over sheet pan

METHOD

Fill a tall saucepan (at least 6-inches [15 cm] deep) two-thirds full with oil. Heat the oil on medium-low to 175°F (80°C). Meanwhile, wash and cut the potatoes into sticks ¼ Ix ¼ x 3 inches (6 x 6 x 7.5 cm) long and place in a large bowl. Rinse under cold running water until the water in the bowl is clear.

Remove the potatoes from the water and drain on paper towels. Pat them dry multiple times with paper towels.

When the oil reaches 175°F (80°C), add the fries in batches and let them blanch for 10 to 12 minutes or until I fry removed from the oil can be broken with your fingers but not so tender that it mashes.

Remove with a slotted spoon or skimmer basket and set on a wire rack placed over a sheet pan. Repeat until all the fries are blanched.

Let the fries cool to room temperature. The fries can be made up until this point and refrigerated up to 2 days before proceeding with the final cooking steps.

Place several layers of paper towels on a large plate or baking sheet.

Reheat the oil to 375°F (190°C) over medium-high heat. Fry the potatoes again in batches, leaving plenty of room for them to move around without touching, about 3 to 5 minutes or until golden brown.

Remove with a slotted spoon or skimmer basket and drain on paper towels. Liberally season with kosher salt or barbecue rub.

STORAGE

You'll need to eat all of the fries—they do not keep well.

A Family Heirloom: Galena Towers' Potato Salad

As with most family recipes, this one from Rod and Sheri Gray of Pellet Envy wasn't written down. This potato salad was first made by Rod's great grandmother, Galena Towers, who handed it down to his grandmother Helen Widler. On one of Rod's visits out to Abilene, Kansas, in the late 1980s, the recipe finally made it to paper. It's very simple but delicious and crowd pleasing.

Prep time: 30 minutes with
    overnight in the refrigerator
Cook time: 30 minutes
Serves: 8 to 10

INGREDIENTS

5 cups (550 g) peeled
    ¾-inch (2 cm) cubed Russet potatoes
2 teaspoons white vinegar
2 teaspoons granulated sugar
1 teaspoon celery seed
1 teaspoon table salt
1½ cups (340 g) mayonnaise

1 cup (100 g) chopped celery
½ cup (80 g) chopped red onions
½ cup (60 g) chopped bread and butter
    pickles
4 hard-boiled eggs, peeled and coarsely
    chopped

METHOD

Place the potatoes in a medium pot and cover with water. Over high heat, bring the water to a boil and then reduce the heat to low. Simmer until the potatoes are tender, about 7 to 9 minutes. Drain and cool for 10 minutes. Place the potatoes in a bowl and toss with the vinegar, sugar, celery seed, and salt. Cover and refrigerate overnight. The next day, add the mayonnaise, onions, celery, and pickles. Combine with a large spoon. Add the eggs. Cover and refrigerate for at least 2 hours or overnight.

STORAGE

Refrigerate for up to 3 days.

Texas

"Like a storybook ending, I'm lost in your charms.
And I could waltz across Texas with you."

— ERNEST TUBB

The Texas and North Carolina regions are in many ways kindred barbecue spirits. In Texas, the focus is beef instead of pork. But that same simple, traditional approach leveraging only salt, pepper, meat, and pitmaster know-how permeates everything great about Texas barbecue. Just like in North Carolina, Texans expect the menu to read a certain way and fusion or out-of-region preparations are, to put it kindly, frowned upon.

Texas is a much bigger state and as a result is a bit more diverse than North Carolina. The Eastern part of the state and urban centers tend towards classic saucy, tender Southern barbecue. To the South and West, open pit–style cooking is common, and the barbecue may be infused with Mexican barbacoa flavors. Our focus in this chapter is central Texas style: beef, sausage, and pork spare ribs seasoned with salt and cooked with oak and hickory.

A lifetime pilgrimage could be spent experiencing the bounty of Texan barbecue restaurants. And while a trip to Vegas or the Caribbean is fun, our idea of a perfect long weekend is flying into Austin, traveling across the region, and eating barbecue 5 or 6 times a day. We start with the new-school places in Austin proper, Franklin, and LA BBQ. Then we branch out to the old-time places like Coopers in Llano; Kreuz, Smitty's, and Black's in Lockhart; and City Market in Luling. If you have yet to experience such a tour, get this on your bucket list.

Can you cook the recipes in this chapter on your Weber Smokey Mountain Cooker or kamado-style smoker? Yes. But to do the style justice, the correct equipment decision is an offset-style pit barrel smoker. The dry, fast airflow environment in an offset is going to create that Texas-style bark. Also, cooking with 100 percent seasoned splits of hickory, oak, and pecan creates the flavor profile required to receive a stamp of approval from a Texan.

Texas expats can be a persnickety bunch when it comes to barbecue and will be quite dubious that a barbecuer in a Chicago suburb or near the beach in LA could approximate the barbecue glory of the homeland. We bet that if you burn a clean fire and follow these recipes closely, you'll impress even the most opinionated Texan.

Butcher Paper Brisket

In many regions, brisket cooks use aluminum foil part of the way through the cooking process to protect the meat and create an unctuous, moist interior—but not the traditional, old-school Texas pitmaster. In Texas, they skip the aluminum foil. The result is a beautiful, crusty exterior that is impossible to achieve using aluminum foil, but the meat is drier.

Butcher paper provides a solution that preserves bark but promotes a moister interior. The butcher paper protects the brisket the way the aluminum foil does, producing juicy meat, but, unlike aluminum foil, the paper lets the steam escape, preserving the crisp crust.

There are only three ingredients in this recipe, so source the best possible meat and apply the kosher salt and pepper separately to ensure even coverage. This recipe is best on an offset smoker burning logs of pecan, hickory, or oak.

Prep time: 30 minutes
Cook time: 10 to 12 hours
Serves: 14 to 16 as part of a barbecue meal

INGREDIENTS
1 whole untrimmed brisket
  (14 to 16 pounds, or 6.4 to 7.3 kg)
Kosher salt
Coarse black pepper
White bread, sliced onions, and jalapeños,
  for serving

SPECIAL EQUIPMENT
Offset smoker
Wood choice: pecan, hickory, or oak
Pink butcher paper

METHOD

Remove the brisket from the packaging and rinse it under cold water. Pat dry with paper towels. Place on a cutting board fat side down. Trim away all of the hard kernel of fat that sits between the point and the flat portions of the brisket. "Square up" the brisket by trimming fat from along the sides, and if the edge of the flat is thin on one end, trim away an inch or two (2.5 to 5 cm) to create an even thickness. Trim any excess fat from the top of the flat but don't worry about the silver skin. Flip the brisket meat side down and trim the fat cap to an even ¼-inch (6 mm) thick. We are not giving portion sizes on the kosher salt and pepper; every brisket is different. With your fingers, sprinkle a light coating of kosher salt on the fat side, then a light coating

of the coarse pepper. Pat with your hand to help the seasonings adhere and then flip the brisket and repeat. Be sure to season the sides as well. If you prefer a peppery brisket, add a bit more. The balance is up to you, but we prefer a light hand with the kosher salt and pepper. Let the brisket sit at room temperature while you get your smoker ready.

Preheat the smoker to 275°F (140°C) using pecan, hickory, or oak.

Place the brisket fat side up with the point positioned towards the hotter part of the smoker. Smoke for 4 hours and then flip the brisket fat side down. Smoke for an additional 4 hours or until the internal temperature reads 175°F (80°C) on a meat thermometer. Tear off two 3 foot (90 cm) pieces of butcher

paper. Crisscross the pieces of paper and wrap the brisket as tightly as possible, securing with some masking tape.

Return the brisket to the smoker and continue to smoke until the internal temperature reaches 195°F (90°C), about an additional 2 hours. The paper should be oily and soaked with brisket fat. Rest the brisket for at least ½ hour or hold in a warm cooler for up to 4 hours. Slice the whole brisket against the grain and serve with white bread, sliced onions, and jalapeños—no sauce, please.

STORAGE

Wrap the room temperature brisket tightly in plastic wrap. Refrigerate for up to 3 days or freeze for up to a month.

Hickory-Smoked Turkey Breast

Unlike most barbecue cuts, turkey breasts are low in fat. That's great when you are looking for something on the healthy side, but that leanness can turn a turkey into a dry piece of cardboard when cooked in a barbecue pit.

The solution is a 24-hour cider brine, garlic butter, and a hotter smoker temperature. Hickory smoke is our favorite. Combined with the brine, it yields a wonderful bacon-y flavor. We cook the turkey on the bone to retain juiciness but a boneless breast works, too. Boneless this is a solid B+, but on-the-bone it can be A+.

Prep time: 30 minutes,
  plus 24 hours for brining
Cook time: 2¾ to 3¼ hours
Serves: 10 to 12

INGREDIENTS

3 cups (700 ml) water
½ cup (112 g) kosher salt
1 yellow onion, roughly chopped
¼ cup (60 ml) maple syrup or
  (60 g) brown sugar
6 cloves of garlic, peeled and smashed
1 sprig of fresh rosemary (or ½ teaspoon dried)
1 teaspoon dried thyme
2 bay leaves
1 tablespoon (10 g) black peppercorns
6 cups (1.4 L) apple cider, cold

3 cups (700 ml) ice water
1 bone-in turkey breast (5 to 6 pounds, or
  2.3 to 2.7 kg), skin on
¼ cup (55 g) butter, softened
1 tablespoon (15 ml) extra virgin olive oil
2 cloves of garlic, minced
1 teaspoon kosher salt
1 teaspoon coarse black pepper
2 tablespoons (16 g) of your favorite barbecue rub with 1 tablespoon (14 g) kosher
  salt and 1 tablespoon (6 g) cracked black
  pepper added to it

METHOD

Place the water, ½ cup (112 g) of kosher salt, onion, maple syrup, 6 smashed garlic cloves, rosemary, thyme, bay leaves, and black peppercorns in a small saucepan over high heat and bring to a boil, stirring occasionally. Boil for 3 minutes. Pour the brine into a 3-quart (2.8 L) stainless steel bowl and refrigerate for 10 minutes. Add the cider and ice water and continue to chill brine until its temperature is below 41°F (5°C).

Place the turkey breast in a large food safe bucket or bowl that will allow the brine to cover the turkey. Pour the brine over the turkey and refrigerate for 12 to 24 hours. If possible, flip the turkey every 6 to 8 hours.

Preheat the smoker to 285°F (140°C) with hickory as your base wood.

Remove the turkey from the brine and set it on a drying rack over a sheet pan. Pat dry with a paper towel.

Place the softened butter, olive oil, 2 cloves of minced garlic, 1 teaspoon of kosher salt, and 1 teaspoon of black pepper in a small bowl. With a wooden spoon or spatula, mix the ingredients until fully incorporated.

Run your fingers under the turkey skin to loosen it, being careful not to tear the skin. Slide the butter mixture under the skin, distributing it evenly over the breast meat.

Pat down your turkey one more time with a paper towel to dry it and then lightly and evenly dust it with you rub mixture.

Place the turkey breast skin side up in your smoker and cook to an internal temperature of 157°F (70°C), about 2 hours. Transfer the turkey breast to a clean rack set over a sheet pan and lightly cover it with a large piece of aluminum foil. Let the turkey rest for 10 to 15 minutes before slicing and serve.

STORAGE

Wrap room temperature turkey tightly in plastic wrap. Refrigerate for up to 3 days or freeze for up to 1 month.

"We Were Just Fine-Tuning the Classics"

by John Lewis

LEWIS BARBECUE

A lot of people say good barbecue is all about the cook, not the equipment. I think it's totally the other way around. You've got to have a little know-how, but having the right tools makes all the difference.

Choose the best meat with the heaviest marbling. It gives you much more room for error.

I first started messing around with cooking barbecue after I moved to Austin when I was 18. I was blown away by the barbecue in Austin, where I made a few different pits out of trash cans and whatever I had lying around. Later—I think I was 28 or 29—I moved to Denver, and I really missed Texas barbecue. I was craving it bad. I started cooking for myself all the time, and then I started inviting people over. The party kept getting bigger and bigger. Someone told me I should get into competition barbecue, which I didn't even know was a thing.

I was on the competition circuit for about a year. I started with one of those double steel barrel smokers you can build out of a wood-burning stove. It worked horribly. Then, I made a smoker out of an old commercial gas oven. It was the size of a one-door refrigerator, maybe a little wider, and all stainless. I welded together a fire box—I was just learning how to weld—and bolted it onto the side. Later, I got a 250-gallon (946 L) propane tank; they have one of the best shapes for smoking and that's what I still use. Everything I did was about trying to recreate what I was getting at those classic joints in Central Texas.

I left competition barbecue when my friend Aaron Franklin opened a trailer on the side of I-35 in Austin in 2009. We used to cook together in Aaron's backyard, long before Franklin Barbecue existed. The cookers we used at Franklin were traditional, but the method was slightly different. We were the new kids on the block, but I was confident in what we were making. As long as that brisket was badass, I didn't think we'd have problems. We were just fine-tuning the classics. Our cooking times were longer. Some of the tricks are trade secrets, but it was mostly about using the highest quality meats. That's the most important thing I can tell anyone about good barbecue: Choose the best meat with the heaviest marbling. It gives you much more room for error.

When I went to La Barbecue in 2012, I built a new pit—my sixth one. Now I'm cooking Central Texas barbecue in Charleston. South Carolina is known for barbecue, but it's nothing like what I do. We heard a little bit of "Go back to Texas," but when we started feeding people, the noise went away immediately. All that matters is what you are putting in your mouth. It has a way of silencing any debate about legitimacy. My dad and I built the pits for Lewis Barbecue from reconditioned propane tanks. It's the same fast air-flow style I've been using for a long time now, but I'm still learning how to cook with the wood here. It's different than in Texas.

Central Texas Beef Ribs

There is nowhere to hide with this recipe. There is no 15-ingredient dry rub or aluminum foil here to save you. The simple ingredients allow the pitmaster's fire management skills to shine. A smoldering or choked fire will come right to the forefront of flavor on these ribs. Burn a clean oak, pecan, or hickory fire, and you will be justly rewarded by the barbecue gods.

Prep time: 30 minutes
Cook time: 8 hours
Serves: 2–6

INGREDIENTS

1 three-bone rack of beef plate short ribs (about 5 pounds, or 2.3 kg)
¼ cup (60 ml) Worcestershire sauce
3 tablespoons (42 g) kosher salt
3 tablespoons (18 g) medium grind black pepper

SPECIAL EQUIPMENT

This recipe is best suited to an offset-style barbecue pit using a blend of well-seasoned oak, hickory, and pecan splits. If using a water smoker or cabinet smoker, leave the water pan dry to best reproduce an offset pit–type environment.

METHOD

Trim excess fat and silver skin from the beef ribs. Drizzle the Worcestershire sauce over the meat side of the ribs and massage it in with your hand. Sprinkle the ribs with kosher salt and then sprinkle with the pepper. Press the rub into the meat with the palm of your hand. Let the ribs sit at room temperature while you fire up your pit.

Prepare your barbecue pit for a 275°F (140°C) 8 hour cook.

Once the pit is settled in, stable, and burning a very clean fire (almost no smoke should be visible coming out of the stack), put the ribs on the smoker, meat side up.

Cook for 7 to 8 hours until a meat thermometer probe will slide into the thickest part of the rib with no resistance. We find the internal temperature of the meat ranges in the 200 to 205°F (approximately 95°C) range when done. Optionally, after 4 or 5 hours, place a bit of aluminum foil on the now exposed bones to keep them from burning.

Remove the ribs from the smoker and let them sit on your cutting board for 15 minutes. Flip the ribs meat side down and remove the center bone. Cut the rack in half and serve these bronto-sized ribs immediately. We choose to forgo any garnish or side dish and simply bask in the glory of one of the best barbecue dishes we know.

This recipe serves two very hungry carnivores, or up to six people if they are sampling

STORAGE

Wrap any leftover meat in butcher paper and refrigerate for up to 3 days.

Pickled Jalapeños

This might be the most-used pickle in our kitchens. We use them in eggs, salsas, sandwiches, Micheladas (see page 128), slaws, and on pretty much anything else we can think of. It's best to always have a batch in your refrigerator.

Prep time: 10 minutes
Cook time: 5 minutes, plus
    10 minutes cooling and a 1-day cure
Yield: About 1 quart (946 ml)

INGREDIENTS

40 jalapeños, cut into ⅛- to ¼-inch
    (3 to 6 mm) rings
2 cups (475 ml) white vinegar
2 cups (475 ml) water
3 tablespoons (42 g) kosher salt
2 teaspoons granulated sugar
1 large clove of garlic, peeled and smashed

1 teaspoon mustard seeds
1 teaspoon ground black pepper
2 bay leaves
¼ teaspoon dried thyme

METHOD

Place the sliced jalapeños in a quart-sized (946 ml) Mason jar and set aside.

Combine the remaining ingredients in a saucepan over medium-high heat. Bring to a boil, stirring occasionally, until the kosher salt and sugar have dissolved. Remove the brine from the heat and let it sit for 10 minutes.

Pour the brine over the jalapeños, making sure they are entirely covered by brine. Let cool to room temperature, cover, and refrigerate overnight.

STORAGE

Cover and refrigerate for up to 3 weeks.

Pickled Onions

This is one of our favorite additions to a smoked brisket or any beef sandwich. The acidity of the onions is a perfect pairing with the deep, sweet richness of the meat.

Prep time: 10 minutes
Cook time: 1½ hours: 5 minutes,
    plus 20 minutes cooling and a 1-hour cure
Yield: Makes about 2 cups (360 g)

INGREDIENTS

1 large white onion, cut into thin
    ⅛-inch (6 mm) rings
¾ cup (175 ml) white vinegar
½ cup (100 g) granulated sugar
¼ cup (60 ml) sherry vinegar
¼ cup (60 ml) water
1 tablespoon (14 g) kosher salt
1 teaspoon crushed red pepper flakes
½ teaspoon celery seed
¼ teaspoon dried thyme

METHOD

Separate the onions into rings and place into a medium bowl.

Place the remaining ingredients in a saucepan over medium-high heat. Bring to a boil, stirring occasionally, until all of the kosher salt and sugar is dissolved, about 5 minutes. Remove from the heat and cool the brine to room temperature.

Pour the cooled brine over the onions. Let stand for 1 hour, tossing after 30 minutes to redistribute the brine. Serve.

STORAGE

Refrigerate in an airtight container for up to 2 weeks.

Michelada

The Michelada is refreshing, session-able, and pairs beautifully with cooking and eating barbecue. Think of it as a beer-meets-Bloody Mary with a little zip to it. We've seen it made with lots of ingredients, such as teriyaki sauce, lemon juice, Pickled Jalapeños (see page 126), and tomatillo purée.

Prep time: 5 minutes
Serves: 1

INGREDIENTS

Kosher salt and coarse black pepper
   (enough to cover a small plate)
Lime wedge
¼ cup (60 ml) tomato juice
1 tablespoon (15 ml) Worcestershire sauce
1 teaspoon Maggi seasoning sauce or Tamari
3 dashes of Valentina hot sauce, or your
   favorite hot sauce
½ ounce (15 ml) fresh squeezed lime juice

1 can (12 ounces, or 355 ml) of Mexican
   or American lager such as Modelo, Tecate,
   Lone Star, or PBR, chilled

METHOD

Mix equal amounts of kosher salt and pepper and spread it on a small plate. Rub the lime wedge on the rim of a pint (475 ml) glass and then dip the rim into the kosher salt and pepper mixture to coat the rim. Set the glass aside.

Combine the tomato juice, Worcestershire sauce, Maggi seasoning sauce, Valentina hot sauce, and lime juice in a bar tumbler or pint (475 ml) glass. Give it a quick stir and then add most of the beer. Give it another quick stir and pour into the rimmed glass. Serve the partially full can of beer on the side.

Red State Sauce

If you must provide a sauce with your perfectly cooked Texas-style barbecue, this is the one to choose. But please serve it on the side. You don't have to use the xanthan gum—it can be hard to find—but it will help to thicken up the sauce without a long simmer on the stove. If you go without, simply shake the sauce before each use.

Prep time: 5 minutes
Yield: 3¼ cups (730 g)

INGREDIENTS

1¼ cups (400 g) light corn syrup
1 cup (235 ml) white vinegar
⅔ cup (160 ml) water
¼ cup (60 g) ketchup
2 tablespoons (26 g) granulated sugar
1 tablespoon (20 g) blackstrap molasses
2 teaspoons yellow mustard
¼ teaspoon ground black pepper
¼ teaspoon crushed red pepper flakes

¼ teaspoon paprika
Pinch of kosher salt
½ teaspoon xanthan gum (optional)

METHOD
Place all the ingredients except for the xanthan gum in a blender and mix on low speed for 30 seconds. Add the xanthan gum and continue blending for 10 seconds. Pour into a quart-sized (946 ml) Mason jar.

STORAGE
Refrigerate indefinitely.

Salt and Pepper Spareribs

After many years of cooking sweet, flavor-bomb competition-style ribs, this has become one of Chris's favorite recipes. Simple and delicious, it really lets the pork and smoke flavors shine. Feel free to use whole racks of pork spareribs and skip the St. Louis trim.

Prep time: 15 minutes
Cook time: 4 hours
Serves: 4

INGREDIENTS

1 rack of pork spare ribs trimmed St. Louis style (about 3½ pounds, or 1.6 kg)
1 tablespoon (14 g) kosher salt
1 tablespoon (6 g) freshly ground black pepper
¼ cup (60 ml) apple cider vinegar
Cayenne hot sauce

SPECIAL EQUIPMENT

Spray bottle

METHOD

With a paper towel, peel the membrane from the back of the ribs (see page 105). Sprinkle the back side with half of the kosher salt and then repeat with half of the pepper. Flip the ribs meat side up and sprinkle with the remaining kosher salt and then the remaining pepper.

Prepare your smoker for a 275°F (140°C) 4 hour cook.

Place the ribs in the smoker meat side up. Keep a steady 275°F (140°C) fire going for 3 hours. There is really no reason to peek, but if you must, keep it to a minimum. Put 2 cups (475 ml) of water and the vinegar into your spray bottle. During the fourth hour of cooking, mist the ribs occasionally and check for doneness. When the ribs just start to break apart when lifted from the center with tongs, the ribs are done.

Remove the ribs from the smoker and let them sit on your cutting board for 15 minutes. Flip the ribs meat side down and slice between the bones. The ribs should have a little tug when taking a bite, tender but with a firm texture.

STORAGE

Wrap room temperature ribs tightly in plastic wrap. Refrigerate for up to 3 days or freeze for up to 1 month.

The Smoke Shop Hot Links

Andy loves hot links, just spicy enough with a big beef flavor. "Just spicy enough" is pretty spicy. In fact, when Andy serves them at The Smoke Shop, people are always a little surprised by how hot they are. Doesn't the name give it away?

This is a big recipe. It makes twenty 4-ounce (115 g) sausages. But it freezes well, so make it all and then freeze half.

Here's a few other tips: When grinding meats, it is very important to keep all of your ingredients and your equipment super cold. It helps the meat emulsify and is a must for food safety. We like to either hang our sausages or cook them on a cedar plank; the direct contact with a metal rack can cook the sausages too quickly or make the casing pop.

Prep time: 2 hours plus 1 day
Cook time: 30 minutes to 1 hour
Yield: 20 sausage patties or twenty 4-inch (10 cm) sausage links

INGREDIENTS

1 tablespoon (4 g) crushed red pepper flakes
2 teaspoons cumin seeds, toasted
2 teaspoons black peppercorns
1 teaspoon coriander seeds, toasted
½ teaspoon cinnamon
¼ teaspoon dried thyme
2 tablespoons (28 g) plus 2 teaspoons (9 g) kosher salt, divided
2 teaspoons cayenne pepper, divided
2 pounds (900 g) beef chuck, cut into 1-inch (2.5 cm) chunks
2 pounds (900 g) pork butt, cut into 1-inch (2.5 cm) chunks
1 pound (455 g) pork fatback, cut 1-inch (2.5 cm) chunks

8 garlic cloves, minced
1 cup (235 ml) ice water
2 tablespoons (5 g) fresh sage leaves, cut into chiffonade
5 to 10 fresh red jalapeños, seeded and finely diced (adjust to your heat preference)
Hog sausage casing soaked in cold water overnight (optional)
Pimento Cheese Spread (see page 61) and crackers, for serving

SPECIAL EQUIPMENT

Meat grinder
Sausage stuffer (if casing the sausages)
Spice grinder

METHOD

Combine the red pepper flakes, cumin, black peppercorns, coriander, cinnamon, and thyme in a spice grinder and pulse until evenly powdery. Divide the seasonings between two medium mixing bowls and add half of the kosher salt and cayenne pepper to each bowl. To one bowl, add the beef; to the other, add the pork and fatback. Mix the meats well with the spice mixture, cover, and refrigerate for 6 to 24 hours.

Before grinding, we like to freeze the meats for 30 minutes until they start to freeze but are not frozen. You will feel ice crystals in them, and they will be slightly hard.

Attach your chilled grinder attachments and with the smallest die, grind the pork and fatback mixture and return the pork to the freezer. With a larger die (no bigger than ½ inch [1.3 cm]), grind the beef mixture and freeze it, too.

Place the ground pork in a chilled stand mixer bowl fitted with a paddle and mix on medium speed for 4 minutes, scraping down the sides of the bowl. Add the ground beef and mix on low speed, slowly streaming in the ice water. Mix for two minutes. Fold in the sage and jalapeños by hand.

If you are planning to freeze any of the sausage, this is the time to do it. Wrap it tightly in plastic wrap and freeze for up to 3 months.

To make sausage patties, roll the meat mixture into 4-ounce (115 g) balls. (The full recipe makes 20.) Form each ball into an evenly flat patty with straight sides. Place on a sheet pan and refrigerate for 30 minutes or overnight. Place in a 250°F (120°C) smoker and cook for 20 to 30 minutes until the sausages have an internal temperature of 165°F (75°C).

To make link sausages, be sure all of your sausage stuffing equipment is chilled or frozen. The meat should be ice cold as well.

Fill the stuffer's hopper with the sausage meat. Press down to remove any air pockets. Lubricate the casing nozzle with oil and roll a casing onto it. Turn the stuffer on the lowest speed and fill the casings with the hotlink meat. Tie off the Hot Links every 4 inches (10 cm). Refrigerate for 30 minutes or overnight.

Place the sausage links in a 250°F (120°C) smoker and cook for 1 hour or until the sausages have an internal temperature of 165°F (75°C).

Serve with Pimento Cheese Spread and crackers.

STORAGE
Wrap and refrigerate cooked sausages for up to 3 days or freeze for up to 1 month.

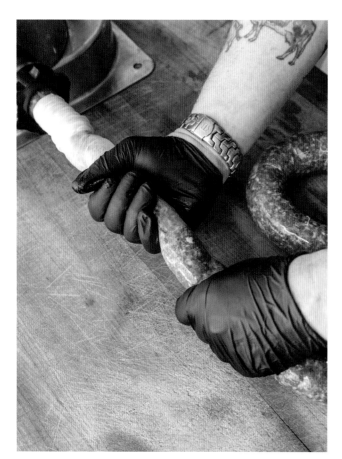

OFFSET PIT BARREL
SMOKER

The deeper you dive down the barbecue rabbit hole, the more likely a ten-foot (3 m) offset pit will end up in your yard. Championship-quality barbecue can be cooked on almost any type of smoker, but nothing captures the primal nature of cooking meat with fire like an offset barrel pit.

This type of smoker features a barrel-shaped cooking chamber with a firebox on one end for indirect "offset" barbecue smoking. This design shows up in many forms: cheap, thin metal backyard versions on the sales floor at the hardware store, homemade pits made from oil tanks, and high-end, competition-grade showpieces. Regardless of where the pit was purchased or how pretty it looks, quality can be judged by one attribute: airflow. It is essential to burning a clean fire and heating up all of that metal. We see many pits where the firebox and the exhaust stack are too small in relation to the size of the cooking chamber. The firebox and stack is the engine of an offset pit. The best offset pits have an oversized sports car engine of a firebox in relation to the size of the cooking chamber.

In our Jambo, we start with two lit chimneys of charcoal briquettes to create a coal base. From there, we add well-seasoned splits of oak, hickory, and fruit wood. No further charcoal is added, and the door of the firebox is not closed until the wood is actively burning. Logs should never smolder, and smoke coming out of the exhaust stack should be almost invisible. Once the vents are adjusted to ensure easy clean wood combustion, temperatures should be controlled by the amount of wood added, not by opening and closing exhausts or vents.

In our experience, it's hard to run a clean fire on an offset pit at a temperature any lower than 275°F (140°C). Don't fear cooking hot. If burning a clean fire requires the firebox door to be ajar and the pit settled in at 325°F (170°C), that is what you should do.

For the el cheapo box store offset pit with a small firebox, the only real option is to use charcoal. The airflow is just not sufficient to cleanly burn logs. Feed the fire with a chimney full of unlit lump charcoal and an occasional ⅛ split of seasoned wood.

Many of the recipes in this book—especially the Texas and Kansas City chapters—are best on an offset pit. It's hard to match the smoke flavor and bark produced on an offset. But these pits are not set and forget. You'll need to eliminate distractions, ice down some beer, and really focus on the art of cooking barbecue.

Bowl of Texas Red

Joe Yonan, author of *Eat Your Vegetables*, used to write fantastic meat-centric recipes before he switched to the dark side and went vegetarian. Andy cooks this recipe often for tailgating—no tomato, no beans, thanks.

Prep time: 30 minutes
Cook time: 2 hours
Serves: 4 to 6

INGREDIENTS

4 tablespoons (60 ml) canola oil, divided
3 pounds (1.3 kg) beef chuck, trimmed of excess fat, cut into ½-inch (2.5 cm) cubes
Salt and freshly ground black pepper to taste
3 cloves of garlic, minced
1 tablespoon (6 g) cumin seeds, toasted and ground
1 tablespoon (3 g) dried oregano
4 cups (946 ml) low sodium beef broth or water
1 can (16 ounces, or 475 ml) of Lone Star or other American lager
½ cup (120 ml) tequila
2 tablespoons (10 g) cayenne pepper
1 tablespoon (15 ml) Tabasco Original Red Sauce
1 tablespoon (16 g) minced chipotle in adobo
1 tablespoon (14 g) kosher salt
½ cup (120 ml) water
2 tablespoons (15 g) masa harina (golden corn flour)
Soda crackers and grated Cheddar cheese, sour cream, and onions for serving

METHOD

Heat 2 tablespoons (28 ml) of the oil in a 5-quart (4.7 L) Dutch oven over medium-high heat. Pat the beef dry with paper towels and season with salt and pepper. Add ⅓ of the beef and cook for 3 to 5 minutes or until evenly browned, stirring frequently. Remove the pieces from the pan as they are browned. Repeat with the next batch of beef, adding additional oil as needed, until all the beef is browned, taking care not to overcrowd the pan.

Return all the meat to the pan. Add the garlic, cumin, and oregano; cook for 2 minutes, continuing to stir. Add the broth, beer, tequila, cayenne pepper, Tabasco Sauce, chipotle, and kosher salt and bring to a boil.

Lower the heat to a simmer and cook for 1 to 1½ hours, stirring occasionally to keep the mixture from burning, until the meat is tender. Add more water if needed.

When the meat is tender, mix together the ½ cup (120 ml) of water and masa harina in a bowl; stir into the chili. Simmer for 30 more minutes until the meat is melting into the sauce. Serve with soda crackers, grated Cheddar cheese, sour cream, and onions on the side.

STORAGE

Refrigerate, covered, for up to 3 days or freeze for up to 1 month.

"I'm Old-School"

by Jamie Geer

When I was a kid, my dad built a smoker out of a great big ol' 40-gallon (150 L) cast iron pot. Of course, we didn't have brisket then; we were cooking shoulder clods. Every Sunday we had a cookout at my grandparents' house. I loved hanging out with my dad while he cooked. I thought it was so cool to play with the fire.

These pits, they are as easy to run as one-two-three.

When I got out of high school, I went to work for my uncle in the welding shop. I was 18 years old then, and I've been welding ever since. One of the first things I built on my own was a smoker. Some guy wanted to buy it, so I sold it. Then I sold some more to my friends. I built my first Jambo in 1989 out of an old underground propane tank that belonged to my grandparents. The metal was all pitted, but I thought it had character. I've still got that original one—I call her "big momma"—and all the pits I make today have that same rough paint job and texture.

That first pit had a damper. I wanted to be able to shut it off so I wouldn't get smoke in my eyes when I opened the door, but it kept moving and the temperature kept changing. I had to get the air flow right. I put biscuits across the grill and I opened the damper. I had to do some "redneck engineering," and I must have gone through 300 cans of biscuits until I finally got it right and the biscuits all cooked evenly. I welded it right then.

Right after I finished making that first one, people started asking for them. I used to build one or two a year, just for fun. I guess I made about 12 pits over those years. Then the economy took down the big sheet metal company where I was working. I figured I was too old to go back on the floor and beat a hammer all day again. That's when I decided to put the pits online and see if I could sell any. I sold five the next day. Within the week, I sold 10. That's how Jambo Pits evolved.

It used to take me three or four months to build a pit. Now I've got a couple of guys and we build a pit every four days, every part, right here. But the J5 style I make today looks just like that first one.

These pits, they are as easy to run as one-two-three. We give people a little thirty-minute one-on-one when they come to pick up their pits—what to do if the wind's blowing from the front or where to put the fires. Everyone has a different way of running them. I'm old school. I put my fire right in the center, with about five pounds (2.3 kg) of charcoal. After the charcoal takes off, I put two logs on, close her down, and let her set in for about 10 minutes. Then I open her up and put the meat on.

A lot of people copy our pits. I used to get really irritated, but now, I kind of feel privileged that I have a product good enough that everyone wants to make one that looks like mine. But there's only one true Harley Davidson . . . and there's only one true Jambo.

Texas Toast

Thick-sliced cheap white bread, aka Texas Toast, is perfect for French toast or a pimento grilled cheese. It's also an outstanding barbecue accompaniment. Serve this rich, garlicky, buttery grilled bread with Hot Links (see page 133) and a few slices of brisket—heaven. Classic or spicy, it's your choice.

CLASSIC BUTTER MIX

Prep time: 5 minutes
Cook time: 5 minutes
Serves: Enough for 6 to 8 pieces of Texas Toast

INGREDIENTS
½ cup (112 g) salted butter, softened
1 tablespoon (4 g) finely chopped parsley
2 teaspoons garlic salt
1 teaspoon finely ground black pepper
6 to 8 slices of white bread

SPECIAL EQUIPMENT
Griddle or 12-inch (30 cm) cast iron pan

METHOD
Mix the butter, parsley, garlic salt, and pepper in a small bowl with a spatula until fully incorporated.

Preheat your griddle to 350°F (180°C) or heat a cast iron pan over medium heat.

Spread 1 tablespoon (14 g) of the butter on each side of the bread and griddle each side for about 2 to 3 minutes until golden brown. Serve warm.

SPICY BUTTER MIX

Prep time: 5 minutes
Cook time: 5 minutes
Serves: Enough for 6 to 8 pieces of Texas Toast

INGREDIENTS
½ cup (112 g) salted butter, softened
1 tablespoon (1 g) minced cilantro leaves
2 teaspoons Fermented Chile Sauce (see page 62) or Frank's RedHot Original
1 teaspoon Worcestershire sauce
1 large clove of garlic, minced
½ teaspoon ground chipotle or ground cayenne pepper
6 to 8 slices of white bread

SPECIAL EQUIPMENT
Griddle or 12-inch (30 cm) cast iron pan

METHOD
Mix the butter, cilantro, Fermented Chile Sauce, Worcestershire sauce, garlic, and ground chipotle in a small bowl with a spatula until fully incorporated. Preheat your griddle to 350°F (180°C) or heat a cast iron pan over medium heat.

Spread 1 tablespoon (14 g) of the butter on each side of the bread and griddle each side for about 2 to 3 minutes until golden brown. Serve warm.

The Jambo Texan Sandwich

Jamie Geer served this sandwich at his Jambo BBQ shop. This is classic "go big or go home" Texas style. It's actually not really a sandwich so much as a tower of barbecue. The best way to tackle it is with your hands: Eat the ribs and then scoop up all that smoked meat with Texas toast.

Prep time: 30 minutes
Cook time: 1 hour
Serves: 4 very hungry barbecue lovers or
   8 regular people

INGREDIENTS

8 slices of Texas Toast (see page 141)
2 cups (450 g) Classic Pulled Pork (see page 25)
8 thick slices of cooked beef brisket
4 thick slices of Smoked Bologna Chub
   (see page 45)
2 links of store-bought smoked sausage
8 pork ribs (cooked and trimmed St. Louis style)
½ cup (125 g) barbecue sauce

SPECIAL EQUIPMENT

4 bamboo skewers

METHOD

In a 300°F (150°C) barbecue pit or oven, rewarm the pork, brisket, bologna, sausage, and ribs until an instant-read thermometer inserted into the center of the meats reads 145°F (65°C), about 45 minutes. When the meats reach 140°F (60°C), warm the barbecue sauce. Then make the Texas Toast.

Once the toast is ready, place 4 pieces on a platter. Evenly distribute the Classic Pulled Pork on the bottom slices. Then layer 2 slices of brisket and 1 slice of bologna on each sandwich. Slice the sausage into 8 pieces and add another layer. Finish off with two ribs per sandwich. Drizzle some sauce over the top and place the other piece of Texas Toast on top. Insert a skewer into each sandwich to hold together. Serve immediately.

STORAGE

Store any leftover barbecue wrapped well in the refrigerator for up to 3 days.

Peach Ice Cream

Chris' wife, Jenny Hart, has a go-to method to finish off one of Chris' barbecue feasts—ice cream! Creative ingredients such as breakfast cereal or herbs from the garden often find their way into the ice cream base. A favorite choice though is seasonal fruit—apples in the fall, stone fruit in the spring, and berries in the summer. Some of the best peaches in the world come from Texas Hill Country, and it's the fruit we think of when cooking Texan style.

Prep time: 3 hours
Yield: 1 quart (946 ml)

INGREDIENTS

3 cups (510 g) chopped ripe peaches (with skin on)
½ cup (115 g) light brown sugar
½ cup (100 g) plus ⅓ cup (67 g) granulated sugar, divided
Juice of 1 lemon
1 teaspoon vanilla extract
2 cups (475 ml) whole milk, divided
4 teaspoons (11 g) cornstarch
1 cup (235 ml) heavy cream
2 tablespoons (42 g) agave nectar
½ teaspoon kosher salt
3 tablespoons (45 g) cream cheese, softened

SPECIAL EQUIPMENT

Ice cream maker

METHOD

In a large bowl, combine the peaches, brown sugar, ½ cup (100 g) of granulated sugar, lemon juice, and vanilla. Stir. Cover and refrigerate for 2 hours, stirring occasionally. Strain, reserving the peaches and liquid separately. Put the peaches and liquid back in the refrigerator to keep them cold.

In a bowl, make a slurry with ½ cup (120 ml) of milk and the cornstarch. In a saucepan, whisk together the remaining 1½ cups (355 ml) of milk, cream, remaining ⅓ cup (67 g) of granulated sugar, agave nectar, and kosher salt. Bring the mixture to a boil over medium-high heat. Cook, whisking constantly, for 3 minutes. Add in the slurry. Return to a boil; continue stirring until thickened, about 5 minutes.

Place the cream cheese in a bowl and whisk in ½ cup (120 ml) of the hot milk mixture. Add the remaining milk mixture and whisk until smooth. Pour the ice cream base into a gallon–size (3.8 L) heavy-duty freezer plastic bag; seal it well and submerge it in a bowl of ice water. Refrigerate until chilled, about 45 minutes, and then pour into an ice cream maker and add the reserved chilled peach juice. Process the ice cream base according to manufacturer's instructions. When the ice cream is set, add the reserved chilled peaches and churn for an additional 10 minutes. Transfer the ice cream to a storage container and freeze until set.

STORAGE

Freeze, covered, for up to 1 week.

The North

"Food is love."
–JASPER WHITE

Believe it or not, there is a vast nation of pitmasters in the Northern part of the United States. And the good ones know damn well that it is not possible to improve on the Louie Mueller beef rib or a Sam Jones whole hog. Glazing a Texas-style beef rib with a Northern barbecue sauce concoction would indeed be blasphemy.

The North does have a growing number of barbecue joints that in our opinion hold up against the best the South has to offer. We'd make the case that New York City is now one of the better barbecue regions in the country. One of the reasons that the city has blossomed in the world of barbecue is its understanding of micro-regional styles. The pursuit of regional accuracy plus the embrace of wood cooking has made pitmaster-driven craft barbecue wildly successful in New York and the approach has spread to Boston, Philadelphia, Cleveland, and Chicago.

The North brings together many types of people from diverse backgrounds. Though barbecue has these strong regional Southern styles, cooking meat with fire is a great equalizer among humans from all backgrounds. After all, wood cooking is a technique used everywhere. In the North, we see Italian, Eastern Europe, Chinese, Jamaican, and Korean cooking styles influencing pitmasters. As Northerners, that is our authentic culinary experience and we embrace it.

Is it required to physically be in Texas to cook great Texas-style barbecue? Well, sure, it helps. And it's certainly harder to achieve barbecue greatness when you don't grow up surrounded by regional traditions. But more and more barbecue enthusiasts in the North are dedicating themselves to the righteous path—cooking with wood, putting in the many hours of repetition, avoiding shortcuts—resulting in some fantastic restaurants such as BT's Smokehouse in Sturbridge, Massachusetts; Hometown Bar-B-Que in Brooklyn, New York; and Local Smoke in Neptune, New Jersey.

Without strict menu expectations, Northern pitmasters can truly harness the freedom to add their own culinary experiences and techniques to the mix. Pastrami, jerk, char siu, kimchi, and other flavors infuse traditional barbecue cooking techniques, creating what is essentially a new regional style. This expansion is very good for the future of American barbecue in our opinion. Check out the recipes in this chapter and see if you agree.

Montreal Smoked Meat

Pastrami at Katz's in New York City and Langer's in Los Angeles rank among our favorite ways to enjoy brisket. Proper pastrami shares many of the same delectable attributes as barbecue brisket—smoke, pepper crust, and a fatty interior. We were recently reintroduced to a variation on pastrami on a trip up North: Montreal smoked meat. The Montreal rendition is smokier and a bit more peppery than traditional pastrami. This recipe requires a bit of elapsed time and a few specialty ingredients, but overall it is pretty straightforward.

Prep time: 2 hours, plus 3 days
Cook time: 7 to 9 hours on the smoker,
   4 hour reheat
Serves: 10 to 12

INGREDIENTS

1 gallon (3.8 L) water
1 cup (224 g) kosher salt
½ cup (115 g) dark brown sugar
¼ cup (20 g) plus 1 tablespoon
   (5 g) whole black peppercorns
2 tablespoons (36 g) Prague Powder #1,
   also known as pink curing salt
1 whole beef brisket (12 to 14 pounds,
   or 5.5 to 6.4 kg)
¼ cup (20 g) whole coriander seeds
2 tablespoons (14 g) sweet paprika
1 tablespoon (9 g) garlic powder
1 tablespoon (7 g) onion powder
1 tablespoon (4 g) crushed red pepper flakes
¼ cup (44 g) prepared yellow mustard
Light rye bread, deli mustard, and Half-Sour
   Pickles (see page 153), for serving

SPECIAL EQUIPMENT

2 gallon (7.6 L) brine container
Meat injector
Spice grinder
Wire rack

METHOD

To make the brine, bring the water to a boil. Turn off the heat and add the kosher salt, brown sugar, 1 tablespoon (5 g) of whole peppercorns, and pink curing salt. Mix well. Pour the brine into the large container. Let cool for 30 minutes and then refrigerate for 12 to 24 hours.

Heavily trim all exterior fat down to ⅛-inch (3 mm) thick. Inject 3 cups (700 ml) of the brine evenly through-out the brisket. Submerge the brisket

in the brine and refrigerate for 3 days. Make sure your refrigerator is cold enough to maintain a temperature below 40°F (5°C).

Remove the brisket from the brine. Discard the brine and dry the brisket with paper towels. Coarsely grind the remaining ¼ cup (20 g) of peppercorns and then the coriander seeds in your spice grinder. In a bowl, combine the ground peppercorns, ground cori-ander, sweet paprika, garlic powder, onion powder, and red pepper flakes

to make the rub. Mix well. Brush the brisket with the yellow mustard and sprinkle the rub on all sides of the brisket. Place on a sheet pan and let sit at room temperature while you prepare your smoker.

Prepare your smoker or indirect grill setup for a 250°F (120°C) 9 hour cook.

Place the brisket on the smoker and apply a heavy smoke for the first hour. For instance, on a Weber Smokey Mountain Cooker, add 3 fist-sized chunks of hickory wood to your charcoal fire. Smoke until a thermometer inserted in the thickest portion of the flat registers 180°F (85°C), about 7 to 9 hours. Rest the brisket at room temperature until the brisket internal temperature is below 100°F (40°C). Place the brisket on a sheet pan and refrigerate overnight.

Preheat your oven to 300°F (150°C, or gas mark 4). Fit a wire rack into a full size 20 x 12-inch (51 x 30 cm) aluminum pan. Pour 1 inch (2.5 cm) of boiling hot water into the pan. Add the brisket, fat side up; the brisket should not be touching the water. Cover the pan tightly with aluminum foil. Cook until a thermometer inserted in the thickest portion of the flat registers 200°F (95°C), about 4 to 5 hours. Add more boiling water as needed.

Rest the brisket for 30 minutes. Slice thinly against the grain, making an effort to keep the crust intact. Serve with light rye bread, deli mustard, and Half-Sour Pickles (see page 153).

STORAGE

Wrap leftovers tightly with plastic wrap and refrigerate for up to 3 days. Unsliced portions can be wrapped tightly and frozen for up to 1 month.

Pickled Watermelon Rind

Prep time: 2 hours
Yield: 2 quarts (1.9 L)

INGREDIENTS

1½ cups (355 ml) water
1 cup (235 ml) apple cider vinegar
½ cup (170 g) honey
½ cup (115 g) light brown sugar
1 cinnamon stick
2-inch (5 cm) piece of ginger, sliced in half
1 teaspoon black peppercorns
1 watermelon (4 to 6 pounds, or
  1.8 to 2.7 kg)

METHOD

Combine the water, vinegar, honey, brown sugar, cinnamon, ginger, and peppercorns in a small saucepan and bring to a boil, stirring to dissolve the sugar. Pour the brine into a bowl to cool for 1 hour.

Meanwhile, carve the rind off of the watermelon, leaving ½ inch (1.3 cm) of fruit on the rind. Save the fruit for the Barbecued Goat Curry (see page 177) or to make Spicy Watermelon Glaze (see page 89). Cut the rind into 1-inch (2.5 cm) pieces and slice off the hard exterior skin of each piece. Fill two quart-sized (946 ml) Mason jars two thirds full with the rind pieces.

Pour the brine over the watermelon rind, making sure they are entirely covered by brine. Add extra water if required. Continue to cool to room temperature for another hour and then cover tightly and refrigerate.

STORAGE

Refrigerate for up to 3 weeks.

Half-Sour Pickles

Our friend Mark McMann of The Little Pig 'n' Potato Pickling Co. here in Boston makes the best sour pickle we've ever tasted. He explains how he created them: "I moved to Boston five years ago and couldn't find a proper traditional, New York deli–style half-sour pickle. This half-sour is a traditional Russian-Jewish–style brought from the Ukraine to NYC in the late 1800s. What makes this pickle different is that it is a cold fermentation pickle which allows it to retain its crunch through the lifetime of the pickle (as long as it's kept whole and cold). It also has a 'softer' spice to it and preserves the flavor of the cucumber while at its peak. After all is said and done, this pickle should taste like a cucumber, just a little more 'effervescent.'"

Mark's half sour pickle—which he calls "It's Just a Cucumber"—was awarded first place in the Judges' Pick and People's Pick categories at the Boston Fermentation Festival in 2015.

Prep time: 20 minutes, overnight to cool brine, 24-hour brine, and then a 7-day cure
Yield: 1 pound (455 g) pickles

INGREDIENTS

4 cups (946 ml) water
3 tablespoons (54 g) table salt
2 cloves of garlic, peeled and crushed gently
2 whole allspice berries
2 bay leaves
1½ teaspoons whole coriander seeds
1½ teaspoons whole mustard seeds
1½ teaspoons whole black peppercorns
½ teaspoon dill seeds
½ teaspoon crushed red pepper flakes
4 sprigs of fresh dill
1 pound (455 g) whole Kirby pickling cucumbers

SPECIAL EQUIPMENT

Wide-mouth, quart-size (946 ml) Mason jar

METHOD

Combine the water and salt in a saucepan over medium-high heat. Bring to a boil for 2 minutes. Transfer the brine to a bowl or quart-sized (946 ml) Mason jar and cool completely. Then refrigerate overnight.

In a separate bowl, combine the garlic, spices, and fresh dill. Rinse the cucumbers and add them to the bowl of seasonings. Add ice water to cover and refrigerate overnight.

The next day, drain the ice water from the cucumbers and remove any leftover ice. Place the cucumbers standing upright in a quart-sized (946 ml) wide-mouth Mason jar. Add the spice mixture and pour the brine over the cucumbers to cover generously. Cover the jar and refrigerate for 7 days. Open the jar and enjoy. Pickles should be stored whole to retain their crunch. Slice them just before serving.

NOTE: Simply double the amount of garlic and fresh dill to make a fine kosher dill pickle.

STORAGE

Refrigerate in a tightly sealed container for up to 3 weeks.

"Barbecue Can Take You to a Different Place"

by Bill Durney

HOMETOWN BAR–B–QUE

I don't have any lineage in barbecue.

I grew up in Brooklyn. My mother could burn toast and my father cooked everything to over well. The saving grace was my grandmother from Norway. She lived in this community and was quasi-raised by an Italian family, so I grew up eating authentic Italian food from my Norwegian grandmother. She was a master cook.

I didn't know what barbecue was until seven or eight years ago. I had no idea that this world I am immersed in even existed. I was in the private security business. We travelled all around the world protecting A-list celebrities. I was traveling in South America and I saw people cooking over open fires. That inspired me. When I was on a protection assignment in Texas, we went to Louie Mueller Barbecue in Taylor. I was one step in the door and I said, "This is what I want my restaurant to smell like." I'd never thought about opening a restaurant before that. That moment changed my life, defining who I was and what I wanted to be.

That's when I started cooking. I ruined a lot of meat. Everybody ruins a lot of meat, so don't start with big stuff like pork butts and brisket. Start with a sausage or a piece of turkey or chicken, something manageable. Light up your smoker and get a clean fire. Cook it through, slice it beautifully, taste it, and—wow. There are no secrets to

barbecue; I'll give anyone my recipe. For a whole hog, I use salt, 60-mesh black pepper, and white oak. I finish it with cherry if I can find it. And it's 14 hours in the pit. That's the recipe—but that doesn't mean it's easy.

Barbecue can take you to a different place. That's what I want Hometown Bar-B-Que to do. For me, though, it's

---

There are no secrets to barbecue; I'll give anyone my recipe.

---

not Texas. It's the streets of multiethnic Brooklyn. It's the smells and sights and sounds I grew up with. What we do here is something completely unique to my experience, just like Sam Jones's hog at Skylight Inn is unique to his experience. Sam can't put Jamaican jerk baby back ribs on his menu. It's not what he does. It's not what his father did. It's not what his grandfather did. But my granddaddy didn't cook barbecue. I get to create something new, using traditional techniques.

We have Chinese sticky ribs on the menu. It's a dish from Flatbush

Avenue, where I grew up. I think that road had the most bars you can fit into a mile and there were just two restaurants open late at night: a pizzeria called Lenny and John's and Kam Fung. At Kam Fung, we'd order Chinese spare ribs with white rice. You had to gnaw the meat off the bone. They certainly weren't tender ribs but there was something about it that was so pleasing. It just worked. It made sense. I wanted to recreate that experience—but better.

I work 90 hours a week here and I never—not for one hour—feel like I'm working. If I could be on the fires every single night I would. That's where I'm at peace. But we're bigger than that now. Every single day we're trying to make the best food we can make. Everybody talks about who makes the best barbecue in the country and everybody has a different opinion of what barbecue should be. That's the beauty of barbecue. We can be part of that conversation.

Hometown Bar-B-Que Chinese Sticky Ribs

This is one of the key recipes that tells the story of Billy Durney's culinary journey at Hometown Bar-B-Que. Cook the loinbacks traditionally with a light seasoning until just tender. And instead of a Memphis-style glaze, hit them up with this glaze straight out of Chinatown. The glaze works well on grilled boneless pork chops or chicken thighs as well.

Prep time: 15 minutes
Cook time: 3½ to 4 hours
Serves: 6 to 8 as part of a barbecue meal

INGREDIENTS

2 racks (3 to 4 pounds, or 1.3 to 1.8 kg each) pork loin back ribs, membranes removed
2 tablespoons (24 g) kosher salt
1 tablespoon (6 g) ground black pepper
2 cups (500 g) Sticky Chinese Barbecue Sauce (see below)
2 scallions, julienned
1 tablespoon (8 g) white sesame seeds

METHOD

Preheat your smoker for 275°F (140°C) using a fruit wood such as apple or cherry.

Sprinkle the ribs lightly with kosher salt and pepper. Place the ribs on the smoker meat side up. Smoke for 2 hours. Brush the ribs with the Sticky Chinese Barbecue Sauce and flip. Brush the bone side of the ribs with the sauce.

Smoke for 1 hour. Open the smoker and brush the bone side again and then flip and brush the meat side. Cook for 30 minutes longer and then evaluate for doneness: the ribs should just start to break apart when lifted in the center with a pair of tongs. If they don't, continue smoking for another 30 minutes.

Remove the ribs from the smoker and brush sauce on both sides. Flip onto a cutting board meat side down and slice between the bones. Pile the ribs on a platter. Drizzle with some more sauce and sprinkle scallions and sesame seeds on top.

STORAGE

Wrap and refrigerate for up to 3 days or freeze for up to 1 month.

STICKY CHINESE BARBECUE SAUCE

Prep time: 15 minutes
Cook time: 15 minutes
Yield: About 3 cups (750 g)

INGREDIENTS

3 tablespoons (24 g) cornstarch
3 tablespoons (45 ml) water
2¼ cups (510 g) packed light brown sugar
2¼ cups (535 ml) low sodium tamari
¾ cup (175 ml) water
½ cup (50 g) diced scallions
16 cloves of garlic, minced
3 tablespoons (45 ml) rice wine vinegar
3 tablespoons (45 g) sambal oelek (red chile paste)
2 tablespoons (60 g) gochujang (red pepper paste)
1½ tablespoons (25 ml) toasted sesame oil
1 tablespoon (8 g) grated ginger
1½ teaspoons black pepper
½ teaspoon fish sauce

METHOD

In a small bowl, combine the cornstarch and 3 tablespoons (45 ml) of water to make a slurry; set aside. Add the remaining ingredients to a saucepan and bring to a boil. Reduce to a simmer and stir in the slurry. Stir the sauce until thickened, about 10 minutes.

STORAGE

Refrigerate covered for up to a month.

"You Can Cook Great Barbecue Anywhere"

by Andy Husbands

I get the question all the time: "Where were born? Are you from the South?" And when I tell them I was born in Seattle, they ask, "Well, did you spend a lot of time in the South?" Nope. And that's okay. You can cook great barbecue anywhere.

A perfect rib is just a really sexy, beautiful thing.

There's a really strong Southern heritage and history to barbecue, and I think it is important to honor it. That means learning from those traditions. That's one of the supercool things happening in barbecue right now. We're seeing really talented cooks from all over the country recognize that this is a craft to be studied.

You don't have to be Thomas Keller. I mean, you don't have to have in-born talent to make great barbecue. I'm not saying you are going to get it right the first time. In fact, I guarantee you won't. You have to practice and practice. I like ribs and I've been cooking them for years. To me, a perfect rib is just a really sexy, beautiful thing. And to get it just right—that's my constant challenge. The smoker is a live creature, and every day is a little different.

My life has always revolved around food. Even in high school, I knew I wanted to be a cook. Chris and I were friends since we were in the same homeroom, and we spent a lot of time talking about food and drink. Later—this is 1991 or 1992—we worked together at the original East Coast Grill in Cambridge, Massachusetts, with Chris Schlesinger. Next door was Jake & Earl's, his barbecue place. I'd had barbecue before, but I didn't really understand it until I started to work for Schlesinger. To eat meat like that, just out of the smoker, it blew my mind. And competition barbecue combined everything I loved: live-fire cooking, great food, a little bourbon, and weekends with my friends. Team IQUE grew out of that.

Chris and I were opening our first restaurant then—Tremont 647 in Boston, which I still own—and competition barbecue was an escape for me. We were doing 10 or 15 competitions a year; it was a passion. That's the coolest thing about the barbecue community: People may not agree about anything when it comes to barbecue, but they are all passionate about it. And they want to learn from each other.

I never thought of barbecue as my business. It's something I do with friends, but now I have a barbecue restaurant in Cambridge, The Smoke Shop. I wanted to share everything that I've learned about this craft in competition and to support and build the barbecue community. I don't think that Boston will ever be as well known for its barbecue as Austin or Kansas City or Memphis. But just like you can find great pizza in Austin or chowder in Kansas City, you can find some damn good barbecue in Boston.

Short Ribs and New England Lobster Roll

We've mashed up our New England backgrounds and love of Southern barbecue into a single bite. This dish is big in all ways: impressive looking with intense flavor. Brown butter is one of the secret ingredients to amp up the lobster flavor.

Prep time: 1 hour
Cook time: 8 hours if cooking Central Texas Beef Ribs
Serves: 6

INGREDIENTS

Central Texas Beef Ribs (see page 125)
¼ cup (60 ml) Worcestershire sauce
¼ cup (56 g) kosher salt
¼ cup (24 g) ground black pepper
2 teaspoons garlic powder
8 tablespoons (112 g) unsalted butter
½ cup (120 ml) vegetable oil
1 egg
1 tablespoon (15 ml) fresh lemon juice
1 clove of garlic

1 teaspoon Old Bay Seasoning
1 tablespoon (4 g) fresh tarragon leaves, roughly chopped
2 teaspoons fresh parsley leaves, roughly chopped
Kosher salt and freshly cracked black pepper for seasoning
1 pound (455 g) freshly cooked lobster meat, roughly chopped
6 hot dog buns

METHOD

Either rewarm or hold your perfectly cooked Central Texas Beef Ribs.

Make a brown butter aioli for the lobster: Add the butter to a saucepan over medium heat. Let the butter melt, swirling occasionally. Once the butter starts to foam, stir it continuously until the solids in the bottom of the pan turn a light, toasty brown. Immediately remove the pan from the heat, pour the butter into a glass measuring cup, and taste it: There should be no burnt taste at all. (If there is, start over with fresh butter.) Add the oil to the butter and allow the mixture to cool for 10 minutes.

Combine the egg, lemon juice, garlic, and Old Bay Seasoning in a food processor or blender. Puree for 30 seconds and then very slowly stream in the butter mixture until the sauce thickens and forms a mayonnaise. (You may not need to add all of the oil.) Add the herbs and pulse in until combined. Place the aioli in a large mixing bowl. Season the aioli with kosher salt and freshly cracked black pepper to taste. Cover and refrigerate.

Place the warm beef ribs on a cutting board. Slice the meat off the bone. Slice the barbecue beef into ¼-inch (6 mm) slices.

Remove the aioli from the refrigerator and fold in the lobster meat.

Evenly distribute the sliced beef onto 6 hot dog buns. Top each sandwich with the lobster aioli. Serve immediately.

STORAGE

Wrap leftover beef and lobster separately tightly with plastic wrap and refrigerate for up to 3 days.

City Ham

An entire book could be devoted to the art of making country ham from a whole pig leg. Our friend John Delpha of Rosebud American Kitchen & Bar in Somerville, Massachusetts, leverages pork loin for a much quicker yet also delicious "city" ham. Cut this ham in ½-inch (1.3 cm) slices for Canadian bacon and griddle with maple syrup and butter. Or slice thin and serve with room temperature goat cheese, warm biscuits, and wildflower honey.

Prep time: 30 minutes active, plus 6 days
Cook time: 3 hours
Serves: 20 sandwiches

INGREDIENTS

1 gallon (3.8 L) water

1½ cups (336 g) kosher salt

1 cup (200 g) granulated sugar

1 cup (235 ml) 100% maple syrup, amber grades preferred

8 teaspoons (48 g) Prague Powder #1, also known as pink curing salt

2 teaspoons crushed red pepper flakes

1 boneless chuck end pork loin (5 pounds, or 2.3 kg)

SPECIAL EQUIPMENT

Hickory wood

METHOD

In a large saucepan over high heat, combine the water, kosher salt, sugar, maple syrup, pink curing salt, and crushed red pepper flakes. Bring to a boil over high heat, stirring occasionally. Cool to room temperature and refrigerate for 24 hours.

Add the pork to the brine. Keep in the brine for 5 days, refrigerated. Remove the pork from the brine and pat dry.

Preheat the smoker to 245°F (120°C).

Smoke the ham over hickory wood to an internal temperature of 155°F (70°C), about 2 to 2½ hours. Remove the meat from smoker and cool on a wire rack for 30 minutes.

Slice into ½-inch (1.5 cm) thick pieces and serve warm. Alternatively, refrigerate and slice the cold ham thinly for sandwiches.

STORAGE

Wrap leftover ham tightly in plastic wrap. Refrigerate for up to 1 week or freeze for up to 1 month.

Hot Links Bread Pudding

The smoky heat from the Hot Links adds a sublime layer of flavor to this classically rich dish. Sesame baguettes have the combination of flavor and texture we prefer for a savory bread pudding, but any type of sourdough bread will do. The vegetables can be changed to suit the season, too.

Prep time: 30 minutes active,
   plus 30 minutes inactive
Cook time: 60 minutes
Serves: 6 to 8 as a side

INGREDIENTS

8 cups (400 g) ½-inch (1.3 cm) bread cubes,
2 tablespoons (28 ml) vegetable oil
4 large eggs
1 cup (235 ml) half and half
1 cup (235 ml) beef or chicken stock
2 cloves of garlic, minced
2 teaspoons toasted sesame seeds
2 teaspoons kosher salt
½ teaspoon ground white pepper
¼ teaspoon dried thyme
2 cups (455 g) seasonal vegetables
   (See suggestions below.)
2 Hot Links, cut in half lengthwise, then
   into ⅛-inch-thick (3 mm) half moons
   (see page 133)
1 cup (120 g) grated sharp Cheddar cheese
2 scallions, cut into thin rings for garnish

METHOD

Preheat the oven to 350°F (180°C, or gas mark 4). Brush a 9-inch (23 cm) square baking pan with vegetable oil. Spread the bread cubes in an even layer on a sheet pan and bake until golden and toasty, about 10 minutes.

In a large bowl, whisk the eggs well. Add the half and half and stock and whisk until fully combined. Add the garlic, sesame seeds, kosher salt, white pepper, and thyme. Mix well.

Evenly spread the seasonal vegetables and sliced Hot Links over the bread. Pour the egg mixture over top and let sit for 30 minutes, pushing down the bread every now and then to help it absorb the liquid.

Bake for 30 minutes. Sprinkle the cheese over the bread pudding and continue to cook for another 15 to 20 minutes until the center is firm to touch.

Remove and let cool for 15 minutes. Garnish with scallions and serve warm.

STORAGE

Refrigerate for up to 3 days.

SUGGESTED SEASONAL VEGETABLES

SPRING: English peas, julienned sweet onions, asparagus slices

SUMMER: Fresh corn kernels, thinly sliced zucchini half moons, lima beans

FALL: Grated parsnips, thinly sliced mushroom, dried cranberries

WINTER: Shaved Brussels sprouts, diced rutabaga, grated carrots

Kimchi

This spicy, savory condiment originates from the other side of the world in Korea, but it pairs perfectly with American barbecue, especially Central Texas–style briskets and sausages. There are three keys to success in this recipe. First, use a kitchen scale to calculate the correct amount of salt: 2 percent of the weight of the vegetables. Second, keep the fermenting cabbage covered in liquid at all times; this may require adding a bit of extra water. Third, seek out the rice flour ingredient. It adds a significant umami flavor that makes it worth scavenging for in your local Asian markets.

Prep time: 1 hour and 30 minutes, plus
   7 to 10 days
Yield: 1 gallon (3.8 L)

INGREDIENTS
1 head of Napa cabbage, cored and cut
   crosswise into ½-inch (1.3 cm) strips
2 bunches of scallions, cut into 1-inch
   (2.5 cm) pieces
2 large carrots, shredded
6 jalapeño peppers, cut into thin rings
1 red bell pepper, julienned
1 green bell pepper, julienned
4 cloves of garlic, minced
2-inch (5 cm) piece of ginger, peeled and minced

2 tablespoons (8 g) gochugaru pepper flakes
   or crushed red pepper flakes
Kosher salt, as needed
½ cup (120 ml) sherry vinegar
1 tablespoon (13 g) sweet rice flour (optional)
Cold water, as needed

SPECIAL EQUIPMENT
Harvest fermentation crock or 2 gallon (7.6 L)
   food safe bucket
Kitchen scale

METHOD
Weigh all of the produce together. Calculate 2 percent of the weight; that is how much kosher salt you need. (For example, if the total veggie weight is 48 ounces [1.4 kg], you'd need about 1 ounce [28 g] of kosher salt) Combine the vegetables, pepper flakes, kosher salt, vinegar, and sweet rice flour (if using) in a fermentation crock. Mix thoroughly. If you are not using a fermentation crock, you will need to MacGyver one: Place some heavy dinner plates on top of the vegetables to push them down and squeeze the liquid out. Let the mixture sit for 1 hour.

In either case, if the vegetables have not exuded enough liquid to cover the contents after one hour, add some cold water just to cover them.

Replace the harvest pot cover or cover the bucket with plastic wrap pierced with a fork to allow the vegetables to breathe. Place the container someplace where the temperature is between 55 and 70°F (13 to 20°C) and out of sunlight; a dark, cool basement is perfect. Let the mixture ferment for 7 days, checking on it every 3 days to make sure that the vegetables are still submerged in liquid. If they are not, add some more water. If you see any mold on the top, remove

it. Around the 7-day mark, the Kimchi will start to bubble, which indicates the fermentation process is complete. Divide the Kimchi into four quart-sized (946 ml) Mason jars and refrigerate.

STORAGE:
Refrigerate for up to several months.

Smoked Pork Shank Osso Buco

Osso Buco is traditionally made with veal and braised in the oven, but we are always looking for new ways to use pork and our pits. The pork shank is perfect for this method. It absorbs the smokiness of the wood and the slow cooking process keeps it super juicy and tender.

Prep time: 30 minutes
Cook time: 3 to 4 hours
Serves: 4

INGREDIENTS

4 pork shanks (1½ to 2 pounds, or
    680 to 900 g each)
Kosher salt and freshly cracked black pepper,
    as needed
¼ cup (60 ml) olive oil
3 cloves of garlic, minced
1 teaspoon crushed red pepper flakes
1 large yellow onion, diced
4 ribs of celery, diced
1 carrot, diced

4 cups (946 ml) red wine, such as a Zinfandel
4 cups (946 ml) Smoky Chicken Stock
    (see page 196) or low sodium chicken broth
2 sprigs of fresh thyme
1 sprig of fresh rosemary
1 bay leaf
1 recipe Mascarpone Polenta (see page 172)

SPECIAL EQUIPMENT

Hickory or oak
Remote thermometer

METHOD

Prepare your smoker for a 275°F (140°C) 2 hour cook.

Liberally season the pork shanks with kosher salt and pepper, pressing the spices into the meat. Smoke over hickory or oak for 2 hours.

Meanwhile, prepare the braising liquid. In a heavy-bottomed saucepan over medium-high heat, combine the oil and garlic. Cook, stirring, until the garlic begins to brown and become fragrant, about 2 to 3 minutes. Add the red pepper flakes and continue to cook, stirring, for 10 seconds more. Add the onion, celery, and carrot and continue to cook, stirring occasionally, until the vegetables start to brown, about 3 to 4 minutes more. Add the fennel seeds, wine, and stock. Increase the heat to high and boil for 10 minutes until the liquid has reduced by one third.

Remove the pork shanks from the pit and place them in a 13 x 9-inch (33 x 23 cm) baking dish. Scatter the herbs around the meat. Spoon the braising liquid and vegetables over the smoked shanks. Cover the pan with aluminum foil. Place the pan in the smoker (or into an oven preheated to 275°F [140°, or gas mark 1]) and braise for 1 to 2 hours until the meat easily pulls away from the bone. A meat thermometer should register an internal temperature of about 200°F (95°C).

Remove the pan from smoker, remove the aluminum foil, and let cool slightly. With a slotted spoon, carefully transfer the pork shanks to a platter and tent with aluminum foil to keep warm. Discard the herbs. Transfer the braising liquid to a heavy-bottomed saucepan over medium-high heat. Bring the liquid to a boil, stirring occasionally, and reduce to about 2 cups (475 ml). The liquid should be viscous and rich. Taste for seasoning; it will need a little kosher salt and black pepper.

While the sauce is reducing and the pork is resting, make the Mascarpone Polenta.

Spoon the Mascarpone Polenta onto each plate, offset a braised shank on top, spoon the sauce over the meat, and serve immediately.

STORAGE

Wrap leftover shanks tightly in plastic wrap. Refrigerate for up to 3 days or freeze for up to 1 month.

Mascarpone Polenta

Polenta is basically grits' Italian cousin: super easy to make and the perfect accompaniment for hearty braised dishes like Smoked Pork Shank Osso Buco (see page 171). The most important part of this recipe is slowly adding the cornmeal as you whisk. This will ensure there are no lumps in your polenta.

Cook time: 40 minutes
Serves: 4 to 6 as a side dish

INGREDIENTS

4 cups (946 ml) Smoky Chicken Stock
  (see page 196), or low sodium chicken broth
1 tablespoon (14 g) unsalted butter
1 cup (140 g) yellow cornmeal
¼ cup (60 g) mascarpone cheese
  (You can substitute softened cream cheese.)
Kosher salt and fresh cracked black pepper, to taste

METHOD

Place the stock and butter in a heavy-bottomed saucepan over medium-high heat and bring the liquid to a boil. Slowly pour in the cornmeal while constantly whisking. Whisk until fully incorporated. Bring the liquid back to a boil, stirring occasionally with a wooden spoon, and then lower the heat to medium and simmer for 30 minutes until rich and creamy. Adjust the heat as needed to maintain a slight simmer, stirring occasionally and then more frequently as the mixture thickens.

Remove from the heat and fold in the mascarpone until fully incorporated. Season with kosher salt and pepper and serve immediately.

STORAGE

Refrigerate for up to 3 days.

The Smoke Shop BBQ Beans

This bean recipe is vegetarian, but adding smoked pork or brisket is always a good idea. We often will throw these beans in our pit for Friday night dinner at a barbecue competition.

Prep time: 15 minutes

Cook time: 30 minutes in a 350°F oven (180°C, or gas mark 4), or 60 minutes in 275°F (140°C) barbecue pit

Serves: 6 to 8 as a side

INGREDIENTS

2 cans (16 ounces, or 455 g each) of white beans, such as navy or Great Northern, rinsed and drained

1 cup (250 g) *The* BBQ Glaze (see page 31) or your favorite barbecue sauce

1 medium yellow onion, minced

1 green bell pepper, minced

1 tablespoon (11 g) yellow mustard

1 tablespoon (20 g) blackstrap molasses

1 tablespoon (15 ml) apple cider vinegar

2 bay leaves

½ teaspoon dried thyme

½ teaspoon crushed red pepper flakes

½ teaspoon kosher salt

METHOD

Preheat the oven to 350°F (180°C, or gas mark 4) or the barbecue smoker to 275°F (140°C).

Combine all the ingredients in a large bowl and mix well.

Pour the mixture into a baking pan, cover with aluminum foil, and place in oven for 30 minutes or barbecue pit for 1 hour. Remove and toss out the bay leaves. Serve hot. These beans are perfect with fire roasted hot dogs.

STORAGE

Refrigerate, covered, for up to 3 days.

Coppa's Barbecue Pig Tails

We are lucky to call James Beard Award–winning Chef Jamie Bissonnette a friend. He is a master of creating delicious dishes from often ignored pig parts. Here, he shares his recipe for pig tails. The Espresso BBQ Sauce is outstanding on all types of grilled meats. The fried garlic, chile threads, and cocoa nibs are fun garnishes, but don't skip this recipe just because you don't have these specialty ingredients on hand.

Prep time: 15 minutes

Cook time: 30 minutes, after you've prepared the Slow-Cooked Pig Tails and Espresso BBQ Sauce

Serves: 4 to 6

INGREDIENTS

1 batch of Slow-Cooked Pig Tails (see page 175)

1 cup (250 g) Espresso BBQ Sauce (see page 175)

¼ cup (15 g) roughly chopped Italian parsley leaves

¼ cup (60 g) fried garlic (available at Asian markets)

¼ cup (60 g) Korean chile threads (available at Asian markets)

1 tablespoon (8 g) cocoa nibs

METHOD

Set up your charcoal grill for direct medium-hot grilling. Grill the pig tails on all sides until heated through, allowing small parts of the tails to char. Cook for 15 to 20 minutes or to an internal temperature of 140 to 150°F (60 to 65°C).

Warm the Espresso BBQ Sauce in a saucepan over medium heat.

When the pig tails are hot, place them in a large bowl and toss with the sauce to coat completely.

Place the pig tails on a platter and garnish with parsley, fried garlic, chili threads, and cocoa nibs as garnish.

Eat with your hands.

STORAGE

Refrigerate in a covered container for up to 3 days.

ESPRESSO BBQ SAUCE

Prep time: 15 minutes
Cook time: 1 hour
Yield: 1 pint (475 ml)

INGREDIENTS

1 medium red onion, julienned
2 tablespoons (28 ml) canola oil
Kosher salt, as needed
3 cloves of garlic, peeled and smashed
1 cup (240 g) ketchup

1 cup (340 g) honey
½ cup (120 ml) brewed espresso or
  strong coffee
½ cup (120 ml) apple cider vinegar
¼ cup (120 ml) soy sauce
¼ cup (120 g) gochujang

METHOD

In a saucepan over medium-high heat, cook the onions in canola oil. Season liberally with kosher salt and cook until tender but not browned, about 10 minutes. Add the garlic and cook until tender but not browned, about 3 to 4 minutes. Add the remaining ingredients and whisk to combine. Bring the mixture to a boil and then lower the heat to maintain a light simmer where the sauce is barely bubbling for 45 minutes, stirring occasionally. Cool to room temperature and refrigerate in a covered container.

STORAGE

Refrigerate for 2 to 3 weeks.

SLOW-COOKED PIG TAILS

Prep time: 15 minutes, plus 12 hours
Cook time: 1 hour
Serves: 4 to 6

INGREDIENTS

½ cup (112 g) plus 4 tablespoons (56 g)
  kosher salt, divided
½ cup (100 g) plus 4 tablespoons (50 g)
  granulated sugar, divided
5 cloves of garlic, peeled and smashed
2 tablespoons (8 g) plus 1 teaspoon (1 g)
  crushed red pepper flakes, divided

2 tablespoons (6 g) fine-ground coffee
3 pounds (900 g) pig tails
½ cup (120 ml) fish sauce

METHOD

In a large bowl, combine ½ cup (112 g) of kosher salt, ½ cup (100 g) of sugar, garlic, 1 teaspoon red pepper flakes, and coffee and mix well. Add the pig tails, tossing to coat thoroughly. Cover and refrigerate for 12 hours, tossing every 2 hours if possible.

Transfer the pig tails to a stock pot and cover with water by 2 inches (5 cm). Bring the mixture to a boil over high heat and then lower the heat to main-tain a simmer. Cook for 15 minutes, skimming any foam that comes to the top of the water. Remove the pig tails, discard the water, and clean the pot.

Return the pig tails to a clean pot and cover with fresh water by 2 inches (5 cm). Season the water with the fish sauce and the remaining kosher salt, sugar, and red pepper flakes. Bring the mixture to a boil over high heat and then lower the heat to maintain a simmer. Cook until the meat is tender enough to pull from the bones but not falling off them, about 2 hours, skimming anything that comes to the top of the water.

Drain the tails, cool to room tempera-ture, and refrigerate at least overnight.

STORAGE

Refrigerate for up to 1 week.

Barbecued Goat Curry

This dish is infamous: It's the one that got Chris kicked off the $50,000 *Chopped Grill Masters* finale. In our opinion, it was creative and delicious. After coming up short on the intense, nationally-televised event competition (the judges thought the TV version was "a little too coconut-y"), Chris asked himself, "What could I have done differently?" In this version, we take our time preparing the goat (on *Chopped* he had to have it finished in 30 minutes) and cut back on the coconut milk. If you don't want to commit to a whole leg, this recipe can easily be scaled for a small roast or even boneless goat meat skewers.

Prep time: 1 hour
Cook time: 5 hours
Serves: 6 to 8

INGREDIENTS

1 tablespoon (14 g) kosher salt
2 teaspoons ground black pepper
1 teaspoon ground cumin
1 teaspoon ground coriander
1 goat leg (6 pounds, or 2.7 kg)
3 large slices of watermelon, rind removed
3 tablespoons (45 ml) vegetable oil, divided
3 large carrots, peeled
½ pound (225 g) chicken livers, chopped
½ cup (120 ml) Smoky Chicken Stock
  (see page 196) or low sodium chicken broth
6 ounces (175 ml) coconut milk

2 tablespoons (30 g) red curry paste
1 teaspoon fish sauce
¼ cup (31 g) roasted pistachios
¼ cup (4 g) chopped cilantro
3 cloves of garlic, chopped
1 tablespoon (6 g) chopped ginger
¼ cup (40 g) Pickled Watermelon Rind
  (see page 151)
1 lime

SPECIAL EQUIPMENT

12-inch (30 cm) cast iron pan

METHOD

In a bowl, combine the kosher salt, pepper, cumin, and coriander. Using your hands, rub the spice mixture onto the goat. Let the goat sit at room temperature as you prepare the grill.

Prepare your smoker for 275°F (140°C). Smoke the goat leg until a thermometer inserted in the thickest part of the leg registers 175°F (80°C), about 4 hours. Remove from the smoker and rest the meat.

While the goat leg is resting, prepare a charcoal grill for indirect grilling (see page 15).

Place the watermelon on a plate and brush with a little vegetable oil. Wrap the carrots tightly in aluminum foil with a drizzle of vegetable oil and a sprinkle of kosher salt. Place the carrot pack on the indirect side of the grill. Cook until firm but tender, about 20 minutes. Grill the watermelon on the direct side of the grill, just long enough to create grill marks, leaving the interior largely uncooked.

To prepare the curry: Place a cast iron pan over medium-high heat, either on the grill or on the stove. Add two tablespoons (28 ml) of oil and sauté the chicken livers for 2 minutes.

Add the stock, coconut milk, curry paste, and fish sauce. Bring to a simmer.

To serve, slice the goat leg and arrange the slices on a platter around the bone. Arrange the carrots and watermelon around the goat slices. Spoon the curry sauce over the goat. Chop together the pistachios, cilantro, garlic, and ginger. Sprinkle the pistachio mixture over the platter. Cut the lime into quarters and squeeze over the goat. Garnish with the Pickled Watermelon Rind.

Bring the platter of goat out to your guests and let them serve themselves.

STORAGE

Refrigerate for up to 3 days or freeze for up to 1 month.

Giant Pork and Rabe Hero Sandwich

When we tailgate, we go all out. We've done several versions of a giant, five-foot (1.5 m) sub. Building this, we become the pied pipers of sandwiches. People gather around and start to drool.

For tailgates, we smoke the pork butt overnight at home and bring it to the event in a dedicated cooler used as an insulator to keep the meat hot. We chop the meat on site when we are ready to create the sandwich. It's a little bit of cooking theater right in the parking lot.

Prep time: 30 minutes
Serves: 20 to 30 as part of a tailgate buffet

INGREDIENTS

One 5-foot (1.5 m) sub roll, split lengthwise
4 cups (900 g) Garlic Fennel Mayo (see page 180)
2 Barbecue Pork Butts (7 to 9 pounds, or 3.2 to 4.1 kg each) (see page 25 for Classic Pulled Pork), kept hot
1 batch of Broccoli Rabe, warm (see page 181)
1 batch of Caramelized Veggies, warm (see page 181)
2 cups (270 g) toasted pine nuts (optional)
2 pounds (900 g) thinly slice fontina cheese

SPECIAL EQUIPMENT

Propane torch (optional)
Two extra-large cutting boards

METHOD

Chop the pork butts well with two large chef's knives.

Place the sub roll, split lengthwise, on your table. (We usually use two large cutting boards positioned side by side.)

Dress the bottom half with the Garlic Fennel Mayo. Top with the pork and then the Broccoli Rabe, making sure to drizzle any accumulated juices onto the sandwich. Add the Caramelized Veggies, pine nuts, and finally, the fontina cheese. Sometimes we use a torch to melt the cheese. Smear some more of the Garlic Fennel Mayo on the top half of the sub roll and set it in place. Slice the sandwich with a serrated knife into 20 to 30 pieces and let your crowd help themselves.

STORAGE

Wrap leftover sandwiches tightly in plastic wrap and refrigerate for up to 3 days.

GARLIC FENNEL MAYO

Prep time: 30 minutes
Yield: 5 cups

INGREDIENTS

1 cup (120 ml) extra virgin olive oil
15 garlic cloves, minced
1 tablespoon (6 g) fennel seeds
4 cups (900 g) prepared mayonnaise
½ cup (30 g) flat leaf Italian parsley leaves, roughly chopped
½ cup (20 g) fresh basil leaves, roughly chopped
2 tablespoons (28 ml) fresh lemon juice
Kosher salt and freshly cracked black pepper

METHOD

Place the oil and garlic in a 1-quart (946 ml) saucepan over medium-high heat. Cook and stir constantly until the garlic browns, about 2 to 4 minutes. Add the fennel seeds, stir well, and transfer to a stainless steel bowl to cool to room temperature. Fold in the mayonnaise, herbs, and lemon juice. Mix well and season with kosher salt and freshly cracked black pepper to taste. Refrigerate until needed.

STORAGE

Refrigerate for up to 1 week.

BROCCOLI RABE

Prep time: 20 minutes
Cook time: 15 minutes
Yield: 6 cups (240 g)

INGREDIENTS

3 pounds (1.3 kg) broccoli rabe, stems removed, crowns coarsely chopped
1 cup (235 ml) extra virgin olive oil
15 cloves of garlic, minced
¼ cup (16 g) crushed red pepper flakes
¼ cup (60 ml) balsamic vinegar
½ cup red (120 ml) wine vinegar
Kosher salt and freshly cracked black pepper

METHOD

Bring a large pot of salted water to a boil and blanch the broccoli rabe for 3 minutes. Shock it in an ice water bath and then drain well. Allow it to cool and squeeze out any excess moisture.

Place the oil in a large Dutch oven over high heat until the oil is hot enough to move quickly across the pan and ripple a little when tilted. Add the garlic and pepper flakes and quickly stir for about 1 minute until the garlic starts to brown. Add the blanched broccoli rabe, mix well, and cook until coated with oil and warm, about 4 minutes. Add both vinegars, mix well, and season with kosher salt and freshly cracked black pepper to taste. Serve hot or at room temperature.

STORAGE

Refrigerate for up to 3 days.

CARAMELIZED VEGGIES

Prep time: 30 minutes
Cook time: 20 minutes
Yield: 3 cups (450 g)

INGREDIENTS

1 cup (235 ml) olive oil
6 yellow onions, julienned
2 pounds (900 g) button mushrooms, sliced thin
4 heads of fennel, julienned
6 red bell peppers, julienned
Kosher salt and freshly cracked black pepper

METHOD

Place the oil in an 8-quart (7.6 L) pot over medium heat. Add the vegetables and cook, stirring occasionally, until wilted and caramelized, about 15 to 20 minutes. Season with kosher salt and freshly cracked black pepper to taste. Serve hot or at room temperature.

STORAGE

Refrigerate covered for up to 3 days.

Ode to Ozersky Sliders

While we were working on our book *Wicked Good Burgers*, food writer Josh Ozersky took us under his wing and taught us a few things about burger cooking. Most notably, he showed us that with burgers—as with barbecue—simple is usually best. Josh tragically passed away and the world lost a jaw-dropping writer and meat-eating aficionado. Here is our homage to Josh's favorite sliders.

Prep time: 15 minutes
Cook time: 60 minutes for the onions;
   30 minutes for the burgers
Yield: 1 dozen sliders

INGREDIENTS
2 pounds (900 g) ground beef, 75/25 blend
4 tablespoons (55 g) salted butter
1 large sweet onion, thinly sliced
Slider buns
Yellow mustard
Kosher salt
6 slices of American cheese, each cut in half

SPECIAL EQUIPMENT
12-inch (30 cm) cast iron pan
Standard sized paper grocery store bag
Platter large enough to hold 12 sliders
An infrared thermometer
Solid face metal spatula
Wooden spoon

METHOD

Shape the beef into 12 golf ball-sized meatballs and refrigerate until ready to cook the burgers.

Place the cast iron pan on medium heat and add the butter. When the butter is melted, add the onions. Cook and stir frequently for 15 minutes. Add a tablespoon (15 ml) of water, turn the heat to low and cover the pan. Cook for 15 minutes, stirring occasionally. Remove the cover, return the heat to medium, and continue cooking the onions until golden brown, about another 10 minutes. The caramelized onions can be made in advance and refrigerated or proceed directly to cooking the burgers.

Lay the paper bag on its side and slide the platter inside. Set your buns and mustard out.

Place the cast iron pan over high heat for at least five minutes or until it is smoking hot. An infrared thermometer should read 500°F (260°C) or a drizzle of water should evaporate violently. If the onions are cool, heat them in the pan for 30 seconds, stirring constantly. Move the onions to a bowl. Sprinkle the tops of the meatballs with about a ½ teaspoon of kosher salt each.

Place three meatballs salt-side down into the blazing hot pan. Flatten the meatballs into burgers with the spatula. Use a wooden spoon for leverage to push the spatula down firmly to evenly flatten the burger. Season the tops of each burger with another ½ teaspoon of kosher salt. Cook for one minute and use the spatula to flip the burgers, working around the edges first so you don't disrupt the developed crust. Add a ½ slice of cheese to each burger. Cook

for 1 additional minute. If necessary, cover the pan for 15 seconds to encourage the cheese to melt a bit more.

With a quick, firm scraping motion, remove each burger and place it on a bun. Add mustard and a tablespoon (10 g) of the onions. Firmly place the top of the bun on each burgers, place them on the platter, and roll the paper bag shut. Repeat for the remaining burgers. Let the last batch of burgers sit in the closed bag for at least 2 to 3 minutes. Remove the platter from the bag and serve immediately.

STORAGE

There will not be any leftover sliders.

Gingerbread Butter Cake

This is a Northeast Philadelphia specialty introduced to us by our dear friend (and the photographer of this book) Ken Goodman. Andy has experimented with variations on the classic and gingerbread was a real winner. The cake layer is pretty spicy, but it needs to be to stand up to the sweet topping. The flavor will mellow a bit overnight.

Prep time: 30 minutes
Cook time: 25 minutes
Serves: 8 to 10

INGREDIENTS

1 pound (455 g) pound cake mix
2½ teaspoons (5 g) ground ginger
1 teaspoon ground nutmeg
½ teaspoon ground cinnamon
½ teaspoon ground cloves
½ teaspoon ground allspice
4 large eggs, divided
½ cup (170 g) blackstrap molasses
½ cup (112 g) unsalted butter, softened
1 pound (455 g) powdered sugar
8 ounces (225 g) cream cheese, softened

METHOD

Preheat the oven to 350°F (180°C, or gas mark 4). Coat a 13 x 9-inch (33 x 23 cm) baking pan with cooking spray and dust with granulated sugar.

In the bowl of a stand mixer fitted with a paddle attachment, combine the cake mix and spices and mix well. Add 2 eggs, the molasses, and butter. Beat until well blended, scraping down the bowl. Beat for I minute on medium-high speed and then spread the batter in the prepared pan and smooth the top.

In a clean mixer bowl, combine the remaining 2 eggs, powdered sugar, and cream cheese. Beat just until blended. (It's okay if some small bits of cream cheese remain; do not overmix.) Spread this mixture evenly over the cake batter.

Bake until a toothpick inserted in the center of the cake comes out almost clean, about 25 to 30 minutes. The top layer should look golden and pillowy and be fully set (not jiggly).

Cool completely and cut into squares.

STORAGE

Wrap leftovers in plastic wrap and refrigerate for up to 3 days.

Competition Barbecue

"You know what my favorite ring is? The next one."

—TOM BRADY

What compels normally sane people to shell out over $1,000 for the privilege to cook barbecue in a 100°F (40°C) parking lot, or in a driving rainstorm a foot (30 cm) deep in mud? If the goal is simply to cook great barbecue, this can be done in the comfort of your backyard.

And while competitions do offer prize money, we could write another book on better ways to invest $1,000 than on a barbecue contest. Case in point, Chris will spend $300 on a gold-grade 22-pound (10 kg) wagyu brisket to compete in a contest where the top prize for brisket is $250.

The financial investment is just the beginning. Most competitors with full-time jobs and family commitments spend the week leading up to the big event visiting multiple supermarkets to hunt and peck for perfect racks of ribs, in a late-night chicken skin scrapping session, cleaning the barbecue pit, and loading the trailer with a 50-item pack list. Then they get into a truck and drive 8 hours to the contest site. There's site setup, meat inspection and preparation, and only now at midnight on Friday are they finally ready to cook. The overnight cooking of pork shoulders and beef briskets usually results in about 3 hours of uneven sleep. Breakfast may be two cups of coffee, an energy drink, and nip of whiskey.

So why invest all of this time and money?

Here's how it happens: A backyard barbecuer starts getting the hang of cooking and more than one guest at the cookout exclaims, "These are the best ribs I've ever had!" There's a barbecue contest later in the summer in the next town over. The barbecuer figures it would be fun, but the "best ribs ever" probably come in 49th place out of 60 teams. Now the barbecuer has a choice: Option 1 is to shrug and keep cooking in the backyard. Option 2 is to immediately sign up for another contest.

We're Option 2 people. Option 2 requires dedication, tenacity, and a lot of practice. Only after the golf clubs have gathered dust, and many, many weekends have been dedicated to perfecting competition recipes, will the winning call finally come. And when the barbecuer gets that first place rib call, the competitive fire is not extinguished—it is stoked. The next barbecue win is always the best one.

The recipes are all here in this chapter. If you are an Option 2 type, get to work.

Competition Chicken Thighs and Wings

In order to procure twelve extra-large chicken thighs, you will probably need to buy two, if not three, family packs from the supermarket and choose the largest pieces. You'll be trimming a lot of chicken for this recipe; save the scraps for our Smoky Chicken Stock (see page 196)

Prep time: 2 hours
Cook time: 3 hours
Serves: 12

INGREDIENTS

2 to 3 family packs of extra-large bone-in, skin-on chicken thighs
12 jumbo whole chicken wings
2½ cups (570 ml) Chicken Injection (see page 190)
1¼ cups (125 g) Chicken Rub (see page 190) or a commercial blend such as Smokin' Guns BBQ Hot Rub, 3 Eyz BBQ Spice Rub, or Dizzy Dust
½ cup (112 g) salted butter, room temperature
2 cups (475 ml) IQUE Sauce v2.0 (see page 197)
½ cup (120 ml) peach juice
½ cup (170 g) high-quality honey, warm
2 tablespoons (28 g) kosher salt ground fine in a spice grinder

SPECIAL EQUIPMENT

Wood choice: cherry
Half-size aluminum pans

METHOD

Remove the skins from all of the chicken thighs. Cull through and find the 12 largest thighs and the 12 largest skins. Save the remaining thighs for an alternative use. (The bones are great for Smoky Chicken Stock; see page 196.) Trim the thighs into uniform square shapes. Remove most of the meat from the back of the bone. Using a paper towel, carefully pull veins from the thigh meat. Scrape the excess fat from each skin; using a relatively dull chef knife, start at the edges and scrape away the fat. Don't get too greedy. If you tear the skin trying to get that last bit off, you will need to toss the skin and start over. The finished skin should be transparent. Wrap each of the trimmed thighs in a scraped skin and set aside.

Prep the wings. Separate the wing into drum, wingette, and tip portions. Save the drums for another meal and the tips for your chicken stock. The wingettes are for this award-winning chicken turn in.

Hold the thigh skin-side down in your gloved hand and inject 1 ounce (28 ml) of injection on each side of the bone. Repeat for all of the thighs. Inject each wingette with 1 ounce (28 ml) of injection. Place the chicken in freezer bags and refrigerate overnight.

The next morning, follow the timeline or the next page for a noontime competition turn in—or lunch.

TIMELINE

8:30 a.m.	Remove the chicken from the refrigerator and dry thoroughly with paper towels.
9 a.m.	Place the thighs skin side down and sprinkle a generous amount of dry rub on the back side of each thigh. Place the wings flat side down and sprinkle a generous amount of dry rub on the meaty side of each wing. Place in half-size aluminum pans and return to the refrigerator or your cooler. Make sure your smoker is on track to be settled in at 275°F (140°C) by 10 a.m.
9:30 a.m.	Flip the thighs onto a cooling rack. Dry the skin again with paper towels. This is the presentation side of the chicken and any moisture will create splotches. Lightly sprinkle the skin side with dry rub. Flip the wings onto a cooling rack. Dry the skin with paper towels. Lightly sprinkle the flat side with dry rub.
10 a.m.	The smoker should be at 275°F (140°C). We like cherry wood for mild flavor and the vibrant color it imparts on chicken. If you are running a charcoal based fire, add two chunks of hardwood at this time. Put the thighs on the smoker.
10:15 a.m.	Put the wings on the smoker.
11 a.m.	Move the thighs to a half-size aluminum pan along with 4 tablespoons (55 g) of salted butter. Cover tightly with aluminum foil and return to smoker.
11:30 a.m.	In a saucepan, combine the IQUE Sauce v2.0 and peach juice. Warm (do not boil) and mix well.
11:35 a.m.	Remove the thighs and wings from the smoker. Put on a cotton glove and then a second layer of disposable gloves. With a gloved hand, dip each thigh and wings into the warm sauce.
11:45 a.m.	Return the things and wings to the smoker or place on a direct low heat charcoal fire for 5 minutes.
11:55 a.m.	Brush the edges of the chicken with the warmed honey. And sprinkle a small pinch of finishing salt on each piece of chicken. Begin presentation.

CHICKEN RUB

Prep time: 15 minutes
Yield: 1¼ cups (225 g)

INGREDIENTS

½ cup (96 g) turbinado sugar
¼ cup (56 g) kosher salt
¼ cup (28 g) sweet paprika
1 tablespoon (6 g) ground black pepper
1 tablespoon (9 g) garlic powder
1 tablespoon (7 g) onion powder
1 tablespoon (12 g) lemon pepper seasoning

METHOD

Mix all the ingredients well.

STORAGE

Store in an airtight container out of sunlight. Somewhere in the 1 to 2 month range the rub will start to lose its vibrant flavor.

CHICKEN INJECTION

Prep time: 10 minutes
Yield: 2½ cups (570 ml)

INGREDIENTS

2 cups (475 ml) Smoky Chicken Stock (see page 196) or low-sodium chicken broth
1 tablespoon (12 g) MSG
½ cup (168 g) agave nectar

METHOD

Place all the ingredients in a container, cover tightly, and shake vigorously.

STORAGE

Refrigerate for up to 3 days.

COMPETITION
FLAVOR
PROFILE

Two of the judging criteria in a barbecue competition—appearance and tenderness—can generally be handled through a lot of practice. Repeatedly cook barbecue meats until you can consistently achieve a very tender bite without the meat becoming mushy or dry. And then make it look pretty in the turn-in box. It's not easy, but it's also not rocket science. Brute determination can get this done. The more heavily weighted of the criteria—taste—is more elusive. We have a two-pronged attack for creating a winning flavor profile.

First, create a one-bite experience. Classic roadside barbecue is built for bulk; customers eat a whole rack or a giant pulled pork sandwich. Barbecue judges are looking at six portions each of chicken, ribs, pork, and brisket in a two-hour window. If you want to get the judges' attention, you'll need to make a big impression in just one bite. When new teams come and ask our opinion on their competition barbecue entries, we often find them to be under-seasoned, one note, or needing salt. Our goal is to create a powerful flavor punch that hits lots of notes: a balanced mix of salty, sweet, savory, spicy, meaty, and rich.

Second, create a flavor profile that is consistently liked. A spicy raspberry chipotle sauce for instance can be loved or hated. Luck into some spicy food loving judges and you may get a call. You also may just as easily earn your first dead last finish. Imagine two judges: one is an old-time traditionalist who prefers dry rub over sauce and likes spicy food; the other is a newbie whose idea of a tasty Friday night is fall-off-the-bone sweet and sticky ribs from Applebee's. Can you build a flavor profile that both of these judges would enjoy? For us, that winning flavor combination is predominately sweet, balanced with savory flavors such as garlic or onion, and then finished with just a touch of heat. Also, a special background ingredient like cumin, cinnamon, or peach works well but should be barely perceptible, just enough to spark the curiosity of the judge. Keep playing with different spices and combinations until you find a winner.

Competition Barbecue Flavor Profile Pyramid

The flavor profile of a good profile is like a pyramid, with the rich flavor of the meat first and foremost at the base, up to just a hint of smoke at the top.

SMOKE
ADD JUST A
HINT OF SMOKE
AS AN ACCENT NOTE.

SALTY/SPICY
SEASON VERY WELL WITH SALT AND
A LIGHT SPICE KICK ON THE FINISH.

SAVORY
AVOID A CLOYING FLAVOR PROFILE BY BALANCING
THE SWEETNESS WITH ONION, GARLIC, AND UMAMI.

SWEET
SWEET WINS. CREATE COMPLEXITY WITH MULTIPLE TYPES OF
SUGARS, SYRUPS, AND GLAZES.

RICH AND MEATY
FOUNDATION FLAVOR SHOULD ALWAYS HIGHLIGHT THE FLAVOR OF THE MEAT.

Lakeside Smokers' Rib Recipe

Mike and Kris Boisvert, the Lakeside Smokers, were a force to be reckoned with on the New England barbecue circuit. They won an astounding 17 grand championships in just five years. Sadly, they decided to move on from competition barbecue to focus on brewing beer. They are greatly missed at Friday night competition parties . . . but not so much missed at awards on Saturday afternoon.

Mike and Kris displayed a lot of the attributes we often see in successful competition cooks: detailed, organized, meticulous, practice-crazed, and, of course, uber-competitive. So it took a while to wrangle their famous rib recipe, which won countless awards including first place at the Jack Daniels Invitational. Mike and Kris have some truly innovative methods they adapted for this recipe.

Don't leave it to chance finding decent ribs the week of your contest. Start hunting for high-quality ribs weeks, or even months, before a competition. Lakeside's preferred brands are Prairie Fresh or Swift Premium. Look for the heaviest, meatiest, well-marbled ribs. The ribs should have straight bones and no shiners.

This recipe is designed for a water smoker, cabinet smoker, or Weber Smoky Mountain Cooker. It certainly can be adapted to other smokers by modifying temp or cook time. You can also sub your favorite commercial dry rubs or use the dry rub recipes in this book. But we wanted to preserve the exact Lakeside recipe for posterity, so here it is.

Prep time: 1 hour
Cook time: 6 hours
Serves: 12

INGREDIENTS

4 racks of pork spare ribs
½ cup (100 g) organic granulated sugar
2 cups (200 g) Smokin' Guns BBQ Hot Rub
4 tablespoons (55 g) bacon fat,
   room temperature
1 cup (340 g) plus 2 tablespoons (40 g)
   honey, divided
1 cup (235 ml) Stubb's Pork Marinade, strained
2 cups (450 g) packed light brown sugar
3 tablespoons (18 g) Cimarron Doc's Sweet Rib Rub
9 tablespoons (126 g) salted butter, divided
1½ cups (375 g) Blues Hog Original BBQ Sauce
½ cup (120 ml) Blues Hog Tennessee Red Sauce
2 tablespoons (12 g) Obie-Cue's Sweet Rub

SPECIAL EQUIPMENT

Vacuum sealer
Wood choice: apple
Cambro insulated food cart or dedicated
   warm cooler

METHOD

Trim down the spare ribs to a St. Louis cut by removing all of the breast bone section below the bottom of the rib bone (see page 105 for instructions). Remove the membrane with a paper towel. Vacuum seal the ribs. Date them and put them into the freezer. Three days before the competition, take the ribs out of the freezer and place in the refrigerator.

The day you plan to cook, follow this timeline for a noontime competition turn in—or lunch:

STORAGE

Wrap room temperature leftover ribs tightly in plastic wrap. Refrigerate for up to 3 days or freeze for up to 1 month.

TIMELINE

5:00 a.m.	Prepare your smoker for a 250°F (120°C) 6 hour cook.
5:45 a.m.	Remove the ribs from the refrigerator or cooler and unwrap them. Lay the ribs out on a large piece of aluminum foil. Dust both sides with sugar. Apply a fairly heavy amount of Smokin' Guns BBQ Hot Rub on both sides. Tent with aluminum foil and leave the ribs out of the cooler. When your smoker is settled in at 250°F (120°C), add a couple of chunks of apple wood.
6 to 6:15 a.m.	Put the ribs on the smoker meat side up.
9:30 to 9:45 a.m.	Take the ribs out of the smoker and brush each rack with 1 tablespoon (14 g) of room temperature bacon fat on the meat side only. On a large piece of aluminum foil, drizzle about 3 tablespoons (60 g) honey, a ¼ cup (60 g) of light brown sugar, a ¼ cup (60 ml) of strained Stubb's Pork Marinade, and a sprinkle of Cimarron Doc's Sweet Rib Rub. Place the ribs meat side down on top of the above ingredients.
	Then add 1 tablespoon (20 g) of honey, ¼ cup (60 g) of light brown sugar, 2 tablespoons (28 g) of salted butter, and a bit more of Cimarron Doc's Sweet Rib Rub on the back side of the ribs. Wrap the aluminum foil up tight, leaving no air pockets. Repeat for the remaining racks and put back into the smoker.
11:00 a.m.	Start checking for doneness. A meat thermometer inserted between the bones on the meatiest area of the rib should read 200°F (95°C).
	When the ribs are done, keep them wrapped and put them in a full-size disposable pan and hold in a warm cooler.
12:00 p.m. (or immediately after chicken turn in)	Make the rib sauce. Warm the Blues Hog Original BBQ Sauce, Blues Hog Tennessee Red Sauce, and remaining 2 tablespoons (40 g) of honey over medium heat for 10 minutes. Remove from the heat and whisk in the remaining 1 tablespoon (14 g) of salted butter. Open up the aluminum foil on each rack of ribs and start glazing the ribs on both sides with the rib sauce and accumulated braising juice in the aluminum foil. Take the ribs out of the aluminum foil and carefully put them into smoker. After 10 minutes, glaze the ribs again with just the rib sauce.
12:15 p.m.	Take the ribs out of the smoker and put them on your cutting board. Lightly dust with Obie-Cue's Sweet Rub.
12:20 p.m.	Start slicing the ribs and pick the biggest, meatiest, juiciest ribs from the racks you have. Arrange them in the turn-in box with a 4 over 4 pattern.

"I'm Just Trying to Cook Perfect Barbecue"

by Tuffy Stone

COMPETITION BARBECUE TEAM COOL SMOKE AND Q BARBEQUE

I had been cooking professionally for 18 years when I got into barbecue. I had been cooking high-end food—hard-to-pronounce, expensive food—and I had this idea that I would be able to do barbecue with ease. I had smoked meats before, but that was smoked duck and smoked fish, not smoked ribs, not brisket, not pork butt. Really quickly, I realized just how freaking hard barbecue is, and that was appealing to me. I had to lose my "chef thinking" for a bit and learn what barbecue was. Then I could come back and apply my chef sensibilities.

My number one goal with barbecue was to get reconnected with cooking. It's very primal. I thought it might be relaxing, too, which is funny because anybody who has ever cooked beside me knows that I'm never really relaxed. I thought I was way overthinking barbecue—and then I found the competition circuit. At my first competition in Lynchburg, Virginia, I was up early with the other stick burners—I love playing with the fire—and I met all these other people who think about barbecue as much as I do. Suddenly, I had all these friends from all over the country and from all different backgrounds.

Competition barbecue is very detail oriented, and so am I. I've earned the nickname "the professor" because of the attention I've paid to the fire. I run a really, really clean fire, and I'm always thinking about how the smoke will taste with the meat I'm using. When I teach classes at Cool Smoke barbecue school, I focus first on smoke and then on tenderness. Those two things are more important than anything else on the competition circuit. People ask me all the time, do you change your flavors based on whether you are cooking in Virginia or New York? I make some tweaks here and there, but generally, no. I'm trying to create a flavor that can be appealing to everyone. The typical tastes of barbecue are salt, pepper, sugar, smoke, and tang. If you like it sweet and your neighbor likes it tangy,

---

I focus first on smoke and then on tenderness. Those two things are more important than anything else on the competition circuit.

I need to find a balance of those things. That's how competition has developed a style all its own—you have to get everyone with this one bite of food. It's an assertive style that is a little bit of a blend of Tennessee and Kansas City. You'll find ketchup and tomato-based sauces and probably a rub with more than just salt and pepper and a precise control of smoke.

I'm just trying to cook perfect barbecue—barbecue that looks and tastes exactly the way I want it to. You learn something new at every competition. You learn not to build your presentation box too early—I had these rocking ribs one year at the American Royal World Series of Barbecue but I mismanaged them, took them off the smoker early and they tightened up— or too late. At the Jack Daniel's World Championship, I put the ribs on later and they didn't get done. I remember being disqualified in a competition in Lakeland, Florida, for a mistake with my brisket. That disqualification taught me to be a better cook. After that, someone showed me how to separate the point of the brisket from the flat, and I realized that there was so much I still didn't know. Even a professor has more to learn. That's what makes me successful in competition.

Smoky Chicken Stock

Competition meat preparation yields lots of leftover bones and scraps. We often buy two to three dozen chicken thighs in order to produce 12 perfectly trimmed thighs. Trim the meat off of any leftover thighs and freeze the boneless meat for future use. Leave the thigh bones meaty and use those for this smoky stock recipe. This stock is an outstanding way to boost flavor through an injection. It can also be used to add moisture to pulled barbecue meats when you don't want to use barbecue sauce.

Prep time: 30 minutes
Cook time: 6 hours, plus overnight cooling
Yield: 8 cups (1.9 L)

INGREDIENTS

1 gallon (3.8 L) water
5 pounds (2.3 kg) chicken parts (any combination of back, neck, wings, or meaty thigh bones)
1 large sweet onion, thinly sliced
8 sprigs of parsley
½ pound (225 g) hickory-smoked bacon
1 tablespoon (14 g) kosher salt, as needed

METHOD

Put the water and chicken in a large stockpot over medium-high heat and bring to a gentle boil. Skim off any foam that develops on the surface for 10 minutes.

Add the onion and parsley to the stockpot. Adjust the heat to maintain a very gentle simmer for 5 hours. After 5 hours, add the bacon to the stock and continue to simmer for 30 minutes.

Strain the stock into a full-size aluminum pan or large bowl sitting on top of a wire rack. Discard any solids. Let sit at room temperature and stir occasionally to release the heat.

Taste the stock. The bacon may have imparted enough salt. If not, add up to 1 tablespoon (14 g) of kosher salt.

When cooled at room temperature to below 100°F (40°C), refrigerate overnight. The next day, discard fat that has congealed on the surface of the stock.

STORAGE

Refrigerate for up to 3 days and freeze for up to 2 months. We separate the stock into pint-sized (475 ml) portions before freezing.

IQUE Sauce v2.0

IQUE Sauce Version 1 found in our book *Wicked Good Barbecue* is a delicious sauce. But man, some of the ingredients were a pain to procure. We often wondered if it was worth it. Over time, we transitioned to readily available pantry ingredients and a more familiar flavor profile. Feel free to get creative with the spice blend and finishing spice components of this recipe to make it your own.

Prep time: 15 minutes
Cook time: 1 hour
Yield: 1 quart (946 ml)

INGREDIENTS

1 cup (225 g) packed light brown sugar
1 cup (235 ml) apple cider vinegar
¼ cup (60 ml) Worcestershire sauce
1 tablespoon (9 g) garlic powder
1 tablespoon (8 g) chili powder
1 teaspoon onion powder
1 teaspoon ground cumin
1 teaspoon Old Bay Seasoning
1 teaspoon fine ground black pepper
2 cups (480 g) ketchup
½ cup (120 ml) maple syrup
    (Dark amber grades are preferred.)
1 tablespoon (6 g) your favorite dry rub or the
    latest hyped-up dry rub on the competition
    circuit

SPECIAL EQUIPMENT
Spice grinder

METHOD

In a medium saucepan over medium heat, combine the brown sugar, vinegar, and Worcestershire sauce. Bring to a gentle boil and remove from the heat. Add the garlic powder, chili powder, onion powder, ground cumin, Old Bay Seasoning, and black pepper. Mix very well, cover, and let sit for 15 minutes.

Stir in the ketchup and maple syrup and return the sauce to a simmer over low heat. Cook gently, uncovered, for 30 minutes. Don't let the sauce boil.

Process the dry rub to a fine powder in a spice grinder. Remove the sauce from the heat and blend in the ground rub. Let cool. Transfer to a quart-sized (946 ml) Mason jar.

STORAGE

Store in the refrigerator for up to 1 month.

Hot and Fast Pork Shoulder

One of the great things about the Jack Daniels World Championship is it brings teams from all over the country together to mingle on the ultimate barbecue battlefield. At a recent competition, we were lucky enough to spend some time with JD and Rhana McGee. Their team—"Wine Country Q" out of Duvall, Washington—has dominated the Pacific Northwest BBQ circuit for the past five years, racking up 16 grand championships. They shared with us their ingenious approach to cooking pork hot and fast.

Prep time: 1 hour
Cook time: 6 hours
Serves: 6 to 8 hungry judges

INGREDIENTS

1 Boston Butt pork shoulder (8 to 10 pounds, or 3.6 to 4.6 kg)

2 cups (475 ml) pork phosphate injection prepared to manufacturer's directions (JD prefers Kosmos Q Pork Injection.)

½ cup (50 g) Classic Kansas City Dry Rub or your favorite competition grade dry rub

½ cup (125 g) IQUE Sauce v2.0 or your favorite competition grade sauce

¼ cup (60 ml) apple cider

¼ cup (84 g) agave nectar

Kosher salt, as needed

SPECIAL EQUIPMENT

18- or 22½-inch (46 to 51 cm) Weber Smokey Mountain Cooker (WSM)

Injector

Propane Weed Burner

Kingsford Blue Bag Briquettes

4 fist-sized chunks of hardwood

Cambro insulated food cart or dedicated warm cooler

METHOD

Place the shoulder fat side up on your cutting board. Trim away any fat directly above the "money muscle"—the tubular muscle that runs across the butt opposite of the shank bone. Don't go overboard; resist the urge to butterfly away the money muscle from the shoulder. Leave all of the remaining fat on this side in place; only trim that which is right above the money muscle. Flip the butt fat side down. Trim any fat and nubs of gristle from the money muscle. Trim any glands and excess fat across the back of the butt near the bone. With the shoulder still fat side down, inject the pork injection in a checker board pattern—12 evenly spaced injection spots. Inject in 4 spots directly behind the money muscle. Move back and inject 4 spots in the center of the shoulder and then 4 spots in the back of the shoulder. Sprinkle with ½ of the dry rub and flip fat side up onto a large piece of plastic wrap. Sprinkle the remaining dry rub onto the fat side, making sure to get a clean even distribution of the rub onto the money muscle. Wrap tightly in plastic wrap and refrigerate or store in a cooler for 6 to 8 hours.

STORAGE

Tightly wrap leftover room temperature pork in plastic wrap. Refrigerate for 3 days or freeze for up to 1 month.

TIMELINE FOR A KANSAS CITY BARBEQUE SOCIETY COMPETITION

6:00 a.m.	Fill the WSM charcoal ring to the brim with briquettes. Power up your weed burner. Blast the center of the briquettes with the weed burner for 30 seconds. Then proceed to 12 o'clock, 3 o'clock, 6 o'clock, and 9 o'clock for 30 seconds each. Nestle in your smoke wood and assemble the WSM leaving the water pan empty—no water. All vents should be 100% open.
6:30 a.m.	Take the meat out of the cooler and place it in a disposable aluminum pan fat side down. Immediately place the pan on the smoker and close the lid. Don't worry about the cooker temperature at this point. JD likes the meat to go on the smoker cold. The longer the pork butt stays below 140°F (60°C), the better the smoke penetration and bark development.
7:30 a.m.	The pit temperature measured at grate level on the top grate should be 300 to 325°F (150 to 170°C).
8:30 a.m.	Open the WSM and check the pork butt. A deep ruby red bark should be formed. Check that the bark is set by scratching at it with your finger. If dry rub easily comes off, keep cooking for another hour. Otherwise, move on to the wrap step.
8:30 to 9:30 a.m.	Warm and mix the sauce and apple cider. Place the shoulder on two sheets of heavy duty aluminum foil. Pour the sauce over the top and wrap tightly in the aluminum foil with no air pockets. Place the wrapped butt into a clean aluminum pan and return to the WSM.
10:30 a.m. to 12:00 p.m.	Poke through the aluminum foil into the money muscle every 30 to 60 minutes with your Thermapen. The goal is an "al dente" feel in the muscle. The pork should have a little bit of resistance, not the buttery texture you'd find in a properly cooked brisket. The money muscle needs this texture so it can be properly sliced. JD finds the temp of the money muscle is typically in the 190 to 195°F (approximately 90°C) zone when the proper texture is hit.
10:30 a.m. to 12:00 p.m.	Once you've determined the pork is done, remove it from the smoker and open the aluminum foil to release the steam. Let it sit on your prep table for 5 minutes. Rewrap the pork butt and place it inside your Cambro or dedicated warm cooler.
12:35 p.m.	Remove the pork butt from the Cambro or cooler and place on your cutting board. Reserve the drippings that have accumulated in the aluminum foil wrap. With a large slicing knife, slice the entire money muscle off of the shoulder leaving about 1 inch (2.5 cm) of excess meat on the back side of the muscle. Slice the muscle into six ½-inch (1.3 cm) slices and place in your turn-in box. Close the lid. Pull the remainder of the shoulder into thumb sized chunks. Identify the 6 to 8 prettiest, most tender pieces and place in your turn-in box. Brush the tops of the slices and the pulled chunks with agave nectar and reserved drippings. Sprinkle with a couple of pinches of kosher salt. Close the box and get it to the judge's tent.

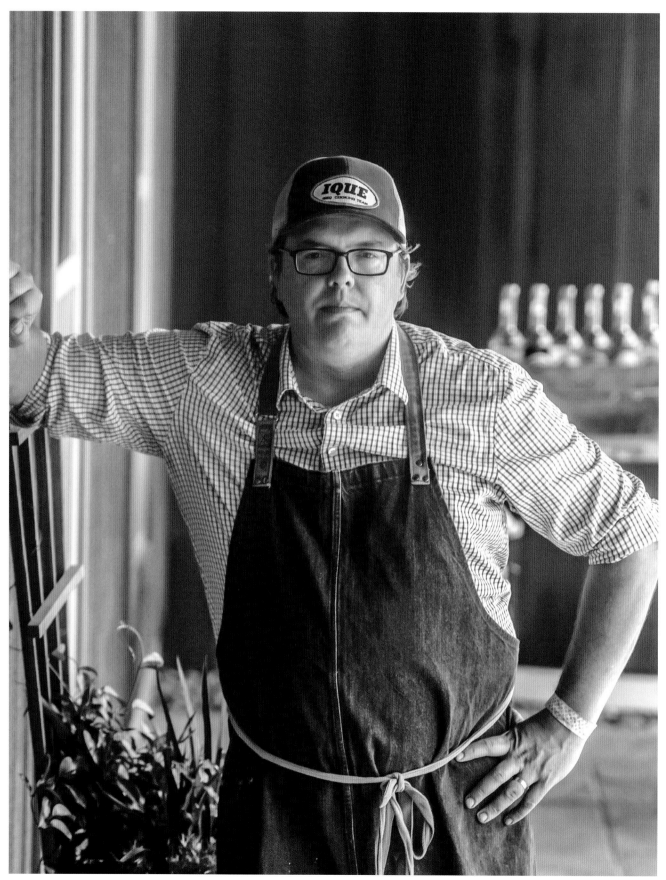

"A Pitmaster is Always a Student"

by Chris Hart

I remember a time when I was cooking 500 racks of ribs in a weekend; they were good. Andy and I were catering and one of the events was also a barbecue competition. Those guys were spending all weekend cooking two, maybe four, racks of ribs. A light bulb went off: I wanted to spend my time and effort cooking perfect ribs like that.

I went out and bought a Weber Smokey Mountain Cooker, the gold standard of inexpensive barbecue cookers. I started cooking barbecue on the weekends: ribs, chicken, brisket, butts. My family would eat it, and when they got tired of it, I invited the neighbors over. They eventually got tired of eating it, too. I was cooking like a maniac.

I developed the flavor profile I use in competition through feeding my own kids and the neighborhood kids. I wanted to find something that pleased everyone—not too spicy, not too sweet, and kind of familiar. That's always been my guiding principle. I want to make barbecue everyone loves.

We started competing as IQUE in 2002 and then we started winning. That sucked me deeper into the world of competitive barbecue. There was one year that out of seven competitions, we won five grand championships. That's pretty tough to do. Then, in 2007, we went to the American Royal in Kansas City.

It was one thing to be winning competitions in the North; in the South and Midwest, competition barbecue is serious business. There were more than 500 teams at the American Royal—some really top teams—but we were bullish, even a little cocky. That first day, the Invitational, we didn't win anything at all. We put our tails between our legs and went back to our camp.

Barbecue is kind of like jazz. Before you can be taken seriously as an improviser, you have to pay your respects to the standards.

We cook a little differently on the IQUE team than a lot of other teams do. Some teams have a set recipe, something they use at every competition. We cook more from the gut. The meat is different every day. It might need more salt or lower heat. Cooking from instinct can be a double-edged sword in competition—you can make a very good decision, or you can make a very bad one.

The next day at the American Royal, the Open, we cooked again. The award presentation started with the sides category: no calls. Dessert category: no calls. Chicken, ribs, pork categories: no calls. Finally, there was the brisket category. They started with the 20th place team and called all the way down to number one. We got the call! The first-place brisket in Kansas City, the home of the brisket.

When I cook at home, I try to pay homage to different barbecue regions. It's kind of like jazz. Before you can be taken seriously as an improviser, you have to pay your respects to the standards. Only then can you find your own sound, or taste. But no matter what tradition you are from or how many competitions you win, you'll never know everything about barbecue. That's the most important thing I've learned: A pitmaster is always a student.

IQUE 180 Beef Brisket

A 180 is a perfect score in Kansas City Barbecue Society contests and over our fifteen—year competition career we have earned quite a few 180s in the brisket category. All other categories have moved through periods of hot and cold, but never brisket. Brisket has always been hot. Almost any subpar brisket result is due to the cook or judging error and not the recipe. This is our classic competition barbecue brisket recipe.

There are a couple of ingredients that may be unfamiliar outside the competition world: phosphates, which improve moisture retention, and a meat cure that helps produce a vivid pink hue to the edges of the brisket bark—known as the smoke ring.

This recipe introduces the method for using injections. There are many mail-order sources of competition phosphate injections available now. Work your way through all of the options in your practice cooks and stick with the producer that provides the best service and a product to your taste. We usually back off of the manufacturer's recommended phosphate-to-liquid ratio and err on the side of slightly under seasoned to avoid overpowering.

Competition rules tell judges not to evaluate the smoke ring, but we think it looks pretty so we focus on producing a vibrant one. We don't want to overdo it—an artificial looking smoke ring is unattractive—we just want to give the ring development a little nudge, especially if we're using a water cooker.

One important step in this cooking process with brisket is flipping the meat: Fat side up to start; fat side down to finish; and fat side back up during the rest. Flipping this way promotes even cooking and retention of fat and juices.

Prep time: 1 hour
Cook time: 12 hours
Serves: 12 to 14

INGREDIENTS

1 wagyu beef brisket (18 to 20 pounds, or 8.2 to 9.1 kg)

3 cups (700 ml) prepared beef phosphate injection (Mix phosphates with water according to manufacturer's recommended ratio to yield 3 cups [700 ml].)

2 tablespoons (30 g) Morton Tender Quick Home Meat Cure

1 cup (225 g) bottled steak sauce or Umami Steak Sauce (see page 211)

1 cup (100 g) Smokin' Guns Hot BBQ Rub plus 2 tablespoons (12 g) ground fine in a spice grinder

1 tablespoon (6 g) freshly ground black pepper

1 tablespoon (9 g) granulated garlic

1 bottle (12 ounces, or 355 ml) Stubb's Beef Marinade

2 cups (500 g) Kansas City Tribute Sauce (see page 93), or Head Country Regular Bar-B-Q Sauce

¾ cup (175 ml) water

SPECIAL EQUIPMENT

Meat Injector

Cambro insulated food cart or dedicated warm cooler

METHOD

Place the brisket on a cutting board fat side up. Using a very sharp flexible boning knife, trim all surface fat from the point section of the brisket. Do not trim any fat that resides above the flat section. Flip the brisket over. Continue to trim all the fat from the point section and continue down a couple of inches (5 cm) underneath the flat. The flat and point should remain connected, but your trimming should reveal them as two distinct muscles. Carefully trim any excess fat on the meat side of the flat but don't go overboard. This fat will render out during the cooking process. Note the direction of the grain. Cut 1 inch (2.5 cm) off each end of the brisket flat perpendicular to the grain. These straight lines will provide a cutting guide during turn in.

Inject 2 cups (475 ml) of the injection with the grain into the brisket flat. Imagine 12 evenly space inject points across the entire surface of the brisket flat. Inject the remaining 1 cup (235 ml) into the point section. Sprinkle the flat with Tender Quick. Let sit for 30 minutes and then thoroughly remove the Tender Quick. If you are at a competition, put the brisket in a full aluminum pan and rinse it a few times with water and paper towels.

Dry the brisket. Brush half of the steak sauce on the fat side and then sprinkle with ½ cup (50 g) of Smokin' Guns Hot BBQ Rub. Get out a roll of 18-inch wide (46 cm) plastic wrap and pull off a 3 foot (1 m) segment, leaving it attached to the roll. Flip the brisket fat down onto the plastic wrap. Brush the with

the remaining steak sauce and sprinkle with another ½ cup (50 g) of Smokin Guns Hot Barbecue Rub. Wrap the brisket very tightly in the wrap. We use an excessive amount of plastic wrap to ensure no moisture touches the brisket. Refrigerate or store in a cooler for 4 to 10 hours. Two cooking methods are presented here: 250°F (120°C) on a water smoker such as a Weber Smokey Mountain Cooker and 275°F (140°C) on a stick burner like a Jambo Joe.

250°F (120°C) ON A WATER SMOKER METHOD:

10:00 p.m.	Prepare your smoker for overnight cooking.
12:00 a.m.	Place the brisket on the grate fat side up.

275°F (140°C) ON A STICK BURNER:

2:00 a.m.	Prepare your smoker for overnight cooking.
3:00 a.m.	Place the brisket on the grate fat side up.

THE REMAINING STEPS ARE THE SAME FOR BOTH METHODS:

5:00 a.m.	Flip the brisket. Sprinkle black pepper and garlic on the brisket flat.
6:30 a.m.	Warm the Stubb's Beef Marinade in a saucepan on the pit.
7 a.m.	The temperature measured in the thickest part of the brisket flat should read 165 to 170°F (75 to 70°C).
	Tear off three large sheets of heavy duty aluminum foil. Place the brisket on the aluminum foil fat side down. Pour the marinade over the brisket. Tightly wrap the brisket. Place the wrapped brisket in an aluminum pan and return to the smoker.
9 a.m.	Check the internal temperature. Typically, we find the brisket in the high 180's Fahrenheit (85 to 90°C) at this point.
10 a.m.	Check the internal temperature. 10 a.m. is our ideal time to hit our target temperature of 203°F (95°C) measured in the thickest part of brisket flat. If you are not quite there, keep cooking until that temp is hit. Err on the side of overshooting the target temperature.
10:15 a.m	Open the aluminum foil and let the brisket sit for 15 minutes.
10:30 a.m.	Tear off three new sheets of heavy duty aluminum foil. Place the brisket on the aluminum foil fat side up. Pour the marinade from the old aluminum foil package over top of the brisket. Wrap tightly and hold in a Cambro or warm cooler.
12:30 p.m.	Remove the brisket from the Cambro or warm cooler and let sit at a room temperature of 70 to 90°F (20 to 35°C).
12:45 p.m.	Warm the barbecue sauce and thin with the water. Grind 2 tablespoons (12 g) of dry rub in your spice grinder.
1:05 p.m.	Remove the brisket from the aluminum foil. With your slicing knife, separate the point from the flat. From the most tender portion of the point, cut three 1 x 6-inch (2.5 x 15 cm) strips. Brush the pieces of the point with barbecue sauce and return to your smoker.
1:10 p.m.	Place the flat on your cutting board crust side down. Remove most of the fat from the back side of the flat with your slicing knife. Flip the brisket flat and brush with the warm sauce. Tent with aluminum foil.
1:20 p.m.	Remove the point pieces from the smoker and cut into cubes. Drizzle with sauce and season with a few pinches of the ground dry rub. Arrange the point pieces in the rear of your turn-in box and close the lid.
1:25 p.m.	Trim the edges to square up the brisket to 8 inches (20 cm) wide. Sprinkle the top with a few pinches of the ground dry rub. Slice the brisket into ¼-inch (6 mm) slices. If the brisket slices are perfect and gleaming with moisture, proceed with finishing your box. If the slices are a touch dry, brush with some of the warm thinned barbecue sauce and remove excess with your gloved finger.
1:30 p.m.	Arrange the slices in a neat row in front of your cubed point. Close the lid, send your runner to the turn-in area, and crack a beer.

Competition-Style Beef Rib Eye

Steak cookoffs are becoming very popular all across the country. We've been tuning our recipes for that type of competition for a while and have discovered a few keys to winning. First is the appearance. You'll need a really hot, meticulously clean grill. And to produce perfect diamond-shaped grill marks, we use thick cast iron grill grates. The standard thin aluminum grates found on a kettle grill will not do the job. Second is flavor, and here is where you can stand out from the pack. We use an umami bomb, a stock reduction with smoked brisket juice, mushrooms, and soy sauce, and a finishing butter for a garlicky, salty sweet cream blast. Third is tenderness. Resting will help the meat relax and evenly distribute the juices.

Prep time: 10 minutes
Cook time: 7 to 12 minutes
Serves: 2

INGREDIENTS
2 boneless beef ribeye steaks,
   1½- to 2-inches (4 to 5 cm) thick
Kosher salt, as needed
Freshly ground coarse black pepper,
   as needed
1 recipe Umami Steak Sauce,
   room temperature (see page 211)
1 recipe Steak Finishing Butter,
   room temperature (see page 210)

SPECIAL EQUIPMENT
Charcoal grill
Infrared thermometer
GrillGrates
Calibrated meat thermometer
   such as a Thermapen

METHOD

Light your grill and get it really, really hot. The grill should reach 600 to 700°F (315 to 370°C). measured with an infrared thermometer. Or you should only be able to hold your hand above the grill for 2 to 3 seconds. Make sure your grill is extremely clean, as in almost new. Definitely check out products from GrillGrates that help create perfect grill marks.

Heavily season the ribeye with kosher salt and pepper. Push a little on the rub to ensure it adheres to the meat.

Give the grill grates one last cleaning with an oiled kitchen towel that you don't mind ruining.

Place the steaks on the grill grates and cook for 2 to 3 minutes. Rotate the steaks 70 degrees and cook for 2 to 3 minutes more. Flip the steak and cook for 2 to 3 minutes and then rotate them 70 degrees and cook for 2 to 3 minutes more or until an accurate meat thermometer reads 135°F (60°C) in the middle of the eye portion of the ribeye. We like an internal temperature of 135 to 140°F (approximately 60°C)

for competitions, though for personal consumption, you maybe prefer other temperatures.

The variance on time depends on how hot your grill is as well as how thick your steak is. Like all wood cookery, a little practice goes a long way, you will get to know your fires, your tools, your meats . . . and it is quite tasty practice.

Once your steaks are cooked, remove them from the grill to rest for 3 to 5 minutes on a wire rack. Spoon your Umami Steak Sauce over the meat and then repeat every minute as it rests.

Keep the steak tented with aluminum foil between bastes. After three bastes with the Umami Steak Sauce, spread some soft Steak Finishing Butter over the steak and let it melt.

You are ready to turn in your steak to the judges or slice and eat. Either way, you win.

STORAGE
Wrap leftover steak in plastic wrap. Refrigerate for up to 3 days or freeze for up to 1 month.

Steak Finishing Butter

Smear this butter on your perfectly grilled beef steak or—bonus recipe!—grill some wings and toss them with room temperature steak butter and a couple whacks of your favorite hot sauce.

Prep time: 5 minutes
Cook time: 30 minutes,
    plus 30 minutes cooling time
Yield: About 1 cup (225 g)

INGREDIENTS
1 cup (225 g) unsalted butter, softened, divided
1 clove of garlic, minced
1 shallot, minced
1 sprig thyme

2 teaspoons garlic powder
1 teaspoon sea salt, plus more as need
1 teaspoon cracked black pepper

METHOD
Place ½ cup (112 g) of butter, the shallot, the garlic, and the thyme sprig in a small saucepan over low heat. Let the butter melt, stirring occasionally, and cook until the garlic and shallots are translucent and soft, about 30 minutes. Remove from the heat, discard the thyme sprig, and let the butter mixture cool to room temperature. It will start to congeal.

Once the melted butter has cooled, transfer it to the bowl of a stand mixer fitted with a paddle attachment. Add

the remaining ½ cup (112 g) of soft butter, garlic powder, sea salt, and pepper. Blend on low speed until fully incorporated. Taste for seasoning; it should be a little salty. Transfer the butter to a sheet of waxed paper or plastic wrap, form it into a tightly-wrapped log, and refrigerate. Soften the butter at room temperature before using.

STORAGE
Refrigerate, wrapped tightly, for up to 2 weeks. Freeze for up to a month.

Umami Steak Sauce

Smoked brisket drippings are a magical ingredient. After resting a brisket refrigerated overnight, those drippings turn into a jelly. We separate the fat and use the remaining smoked brisket jus in sauces and gravies. (Freeze it in ice cube trays until you need it.) You can sub in a beef bouillon cube in a pinch.

Cook time: 1 hour
Yield: About 1 cup (235 ml)

INGREDIENTS

2 portabella mushroom caps

1 tablespoon (15 ml) of extra virgin olive oil

10 cups (2.4 L) homemade beef stock or low sodium store bought beef broth

½ cup (120 ml) smoked brisket jus or 1 beef bouillon cube diluted in ½ cup (120 ml) of warm water

¼ pound (115 g) barbecue brisket, ideally chopped barky pieces (optional)

1 clove of garlic, smashed

1 tablespoon (15 ml) soy sauce

2 tablespoons (28 ml) lemon juice, divided

METHOD

Preheat the oven to 325°F (170°C, or gas mark 3). Place a frying pan over medium-high heat. Add the oil and then the mushroom caps to the pan. Move the pan to the oven and roast the caps for 15 minutes. Remove the pan from the oven and chop the mushrooms. Combine all the ingredients and half of the lemon juice in a saucepan over medium-high heat. Bring to a boil and simmer until reduced to 1 cup (235 ml). Strain through a fine sieve or cheesecloth. Let cool and taste for seasoning. It should have a slight tang but not be tart; add the remaining 1 tablespoon (15 ml) of lemon juice as needed. Use at room temperature.

STORAGE

Refrigerate in a covered container for up to 2 weeks.

Brendan's First Place Sausage

Sausage is a common category on the New England Barbecue Society competition grilling circuit. When the IQUE team first started out, the chefs on the team would often use fancy ingredients (like curry infused hollandaise sauce) the judges didn't care for. Brendan Burek's team, Transformer BBQ, learned that lesson quickly and provided classic, familiar, and delicious flavors that the judges consistently enjoyed. Here is his recipe that won many awards over the years.

Prep time: 1 hour
Cook time: 1 hour
Serves: 12

INGREDIENTS

1 pound (455 g) block Colby cheese
1 pound (455 g) bulk breakfast sausage
1 pound (455 g) hot Italian sausage, removed from casing
1 small sweet red bell pepper, roasted, peeled, seeded, and diced
½ of a jalapeño pepper, seeded and minced
⅔ cup (170 g) Blues Hog Tennessee Red Sauce
⅓ cup (80 ml) maple syrup
½ cup (112 g) salted butter, melted
12 slider-sized potato rolls

SPECIAL EQUIPMENT

Charcoal grill

METHOD

Cut the Colby cheese block in half. Cube up half the cheese into ½-inch (1.3 cm) pieces. Slice the remaining cheese into 12 thin slices. Combine the sausage meats, diced cheese, red bell pepper, and jalapeño pepper in a large bowl. Mix completely but don't overwork. Form 12 patties that will fit roughly to the size of the slider buns and refrigerate for 30 minutes.

Prepare your charcoal grill for two-zone cooking. Blend together the Blues Hog Tennessee Red Sauce and maple syrup and set aside. Melt the butter in a wide mixing bowl. Dip the cut side of each roll into the butter. Grill both sides of the buttered rolls until grill marks appear. Work in batches and grill on the edge of the hot zone, being very careful not to burn the buns. Set the grilled buns aside.

Grill the sausage patties on the hot side of the grill about 3 minutes per side. Move the sausages to cool side of the grill and brush with the maple syrup–Blues Hog Tennessee Red Sauce mixture. Cover the grill. Check the internal temperature of the sausage every few minutes and flip them, brushing with sauce each time. When the sausages reach 155°F (70°C), after about 30 minutes, add a slice of cheese to each patty. Cover the grill and cook until the sausages reach 165°F (75°C), about 10 minutes longer. Place the finished sausages on the grilled buns and serve.

STORAGE

Refrigerate leftover sausage sandwiches for up to 3 days.

Sonoran Hot Dogs

A critical part of competition barbecue is staying well nourished. Throw this on the pit for an hour for a midnight snack.

Prep time: 15 minutes
Cook time: 45 minutes to 1 hour
Yield: 4 big hot dogs

INGREDIENTS

4 Pearl All Beef Franks
(4 ounces, or 115 g each)
4 thick slices of hickory smoked bacon, or
your favorite bacon
4 sub rolls (6- to 8-inches
[15 to 20 cm] long each), not presliced,
lightly toasted right before using
Kewpie Mayonnaise

1 cup (80 g) chopped Kimchi
(see page 169), or store bought
½ cup (90 g) diced ripe tomato
½ cup (80 g) diced yellow onion
¼ cup (52 g) Pickled Jalapeños
(see page 126), or store bought

METHOD

Prepare your smoker for a 275 to 300°F (140 to 150°C) 1 hour cook.

Starting at one end, carefully wrap one slice of bacon around one hot dog, spiraling toward the other end. Insert a toothpick at each end so the bacon stays attached to the hot dog. Repeat with the remaining hot dogs and bacon. Place in your preheated smoker until the bacon is crisped, about 45 minutes to 1 hour, flipping at the 30 minute mark.

When the hot dogs are done, remove the toothpicks. Hollow out some of the soft bread of the sub rolls. Liberally squirt some Kewpie Mayonnaise in the bottoms (along the bottom point of the wedge) and then spread the Kimchi, tomato, onion, and Pickled Jalapeños among the rolls. Place the hot dogs on top and drizzle with more Kewpie Mayonnaise. Serve immediately.

STORAGE

Refrigerate for up to 3 days or freeze for up to 1 month.

Palomas for a Crowd

In addition to your wagyu brisket and finishing dry rubs, a must-have on your competition packing list is cocktail ingredients. The Paloma is tart and refreshing, perfect for outdoor cooking in warm weather. Here is a rendition that produces plenty to share with your friends and neighbors.

Prep time: 10 minutes
Yield: About 20 cocktails

INGREDIENTS
12 limes
5 oranges
4 grapefruits
8 teaspoons kosher salt
1 bottle (750 ml) of tequila
6 cans (12 ounces, or 355 ml each)
   grapefruit soda

METHOD
Juice all fruit (straining out pulp) into a large pitcher. Add the kosher salt and tequila and stir well to combine. Pour 3 ounces (90 ml) over ice into glasses and top with 2 ounces (60 ml) of grapefruit soda.

Meat @ Slim's Tiramisu

Stephen Eastridge, pitmaster of the Meat @ Slim's barbecue team, has rolled this dessert out at both The Jack and Harpoon contests and done very well. Adding Kahlua and mascarpone to Twinkies creates a surprisingly elegant dish without too much effort.

Prep time: 1 hour
Serves: 6 to 8

INGREDIENTS

1 cup (235 ml) water
¾ cup (144 g) superfine sugar, divided
⅓ cup (80 ml) strong coffee
3 tablespoons (45 ml) Kahlúa coffee flavored liqueur
1 pound (455 g) mascarpone cheese
1½ cups (355 ml) heavy whipping cream
10 Twinkies, frozen
Cocoa powder
Chocolate-covered coffee beans (optional)

METHOD

Neatly line a 9 x 5-inch (23 x 13 cm) loaf pan with 2 pieces of heavy duty aluminum foil: one running lengthwise and the other widthwise. The aluminum foil should extend over the edges of the pan on all sides.

Boil 1 cup (235 ml) of water on the stove and remove from the heat. Add ½ cup (96 g) of superfine sugar to the water and mix until the sugar is dissolved. Let cool and then add the coffee and Kahlúa. Mix and set aside to cool.

Combine the mascarpone, vanilla, and remaining ¼ cup (48 g) of superfine sugar in a large bowl and beat with a hand mixer until smooth. In another large bowl, beat the heavy cream until it holds stiff peaks. Gently fold the mascarpone mixture into the whipped cream.

Cut the frozen Twinkies in half lengthwise from the side. Line the loaf pan with the tops of the Twinkies cream side up fitting them snugly in a single layer. Pour half of the Kahlúa mixture over the Twinkies so that they have a nice even brown color. Spread the mascarpone filling evenly over the Twinkies.

Next, place the Twinkie bottoms cream side down in a single layer on top of the mascarpone, squeezing to fit as needed. Pour the remaining Kahlua mixture over the top.

Cover with plastic wrap and refrigerate at least 3 hours or overnight. If you are in a field at a barbecue contest, wrap with lots of plastic wrap, then with aluminum foil, and pack tightly in ice.

To serve, pull the tiramisu out of the loaf pan by pulling the edges of the aluminum foil. Dust with cocoa powder. Slice and garnish with chocolate-covered coffee beans.

STORAGE

Refrigerate, covered, for 1 day.

Acknowledgments

April White for her writing, editing, encouragement, and her tireless efforts to consistently capture the voices of the pitmasters in this book.

Ken Goodman for his friendship and photographic genius.

Amy Mills for her guidance and assistance with the development of this book.

To the pitmasters, Stephen Raichlen, Sam Jones, Elizabeth Karmel, Jake Jacobs, Rod Gray, Jamie Geer, John Lewis, Billy Durney, Tuffy Stone, and Mike Mills, thank you for the inspiration.

Joy Richards for teaching us how to mix a proper cocktail.

John Delpha, Jamie Bissonnette, Mike Boisvert, Brendan Burek, Chris Prieto, Stephen Eastridge, JD and Rhana McGee, Mark McMann, Mark Ballard, Josh Misiph, and Nancy Hart Shean for recipe development.

Nancy Boyce for her laser sharp editing skills.

Todd Ferillo, Dave Frary, Chris Sargent, Jamie Hart, Ed Roach, Eric Simon, the kitchen staff at Tremont 647, Sorel Husbands Denholtz, Melissa Cawley, Michael Pelletier, Chris Clegg, and Chris Sargent for recipe testing.

Thank you Ian Grossman, The Enriquez Family, The Denholtz Family, The Wales Family, Harriet Husbands, Nick Stoddard, Jorge Ruiz, Brian Hammerer, Andrea Pyenson, Joe Yonan, Mark and Laura of Black Coffee Brand Development, Molly Dwyer, Webb Chappell, Lacey Tokash, The Smoke Shop BBQ Team, Neal & Julia of Good Life Productions, Mary Bouxsein, and Ed Doyle of Real Food Consulting.

Andy would like to thank Chris Hart for the hard work he put into this book and the friendship since high school. And Brian and Jana Lesser for the awesome opportunity and partnership.

Chris would like to thank his family, Jenny, Ethan, Jaimie, Riley, Jamie, Sydney, Skip, and Glo for the unwavering love and support. Thank you Andy for the friendship and writing partnership.

About the Authors

ANDY HUSBANDS

Award-winning pit master Andy Husbands began developing his own unique style of cooking upon opening Boston's Tremont 647 in 1996 and later, Sister Sorel. His latest culinary venture, The Smoke Shop, culminates Husbands' continued success and pays homage to his extensive background in the competitive barbecue circuit.

Husbands' honest, approachable fare has earned him praise from *The Boston Globe*, *Boston Magazine*, *Wine Spectator*, *Star Chefs*, and others. He has competed on the sixth season of FOX Television Network's fiery *Hell's Kitchen* and is internationally-recognized for his BBQ team IQUE BBQ, who became the first New England team to win the World Champions of BBQ title in 2009 at the Jack Daniels World Championship in Tennessee.

He is a contributor to Share Our Strength, an active board member of the Massachusetts Restaurant Association who acknowledged him as the 2014 Chef of the Year, and a Rodman Celebration Restaurant Chair. He has also co-authored several cookbooks including *Wicked Good Burgers*, *Wicked Good BBQ*, *Grill to Perfection*, and *The Fearless Chef*.

CHRIS HART

Winner of the Jack Daniel's Invitational World Championship in 2009, Hart has dominated the competition barbecue circuit for the past 15 years with his team, IQUE. The team was the first group of New Englanders in barbecue history to win a World Championship. Chris spends his days developing software, but his passion for cooking barbecue has him following the competition barbecue trail on weekends, pitting his talents against the best pitmasters in the U.S. Chris has cooked multiple barbecue tasting dinners at the James Beard House in NYC. He has appeared on the TV show *BBQ Pitmasters*, and is a Food Network *Chopped* Champion.

Andy and Chris are the authors of *Wicked Good Barbecue*, *Wicked Good Burgers*, and *Grill to Perfection*.

About the Photographer

KEN GOODMAN

Prior to his photography career, Ken spent 20 years in the restaurant industry as a classically trained chef and restaurant consultant with a culinary degree from Johnson & Wales University. Ken's passion for food and music photography has placed him in a national spotlight with clients such as Mario Batali, the James Beard Foundation, Bocuse d'Or USA, *Food & Wine Magazine*, Jane's Addiction, U2, and the Red Hot Chili Peppers. Ken's images have appeared in publications such as *Rolling Stone* magazine, *The Wall Street Journal*, *Hamptons Magazine*, *Edible Manhattan*, *Art Culinaire*, and nearly 25 cookbooks. Ken lives in Nyack, New York, with his beautiful wife Jessica and their two children. When not on assignment, he is likely at home and enjoying their company.

Index